CW00664542

The Fizz Buzz Fix

Secrets to Thinking Like
an Experienced Software Developer

by Edward Barnard

php[architect] anthology

The Fizz Buzz Fix:
Secrets to Thinking Like an Experienced Software Developer

Contents Copyright ©2016–2018 Edward Barnard—All Rights Reserved

Book and cover layout, design and text Copyright ©2020 musketeers.me, LLC. and its predecessors—All Rights Reserved. Print and Digital copies available from https://www.phparch.com/books/.

php[architect] edition published: April 2020

Print ISBN:	978-1-940111-75-9
PDF ISBN:	978-1-940111-76-6
ePub ISBN:	978-1-940111-77-3
Mobi ISBN	978-1-940111-78-0

Produced & Printed in the United States

No part of this book may be reproduced, stored in a public retrieval system, or publicly transmitted in any form or by means without the prior written permission of the publisher, except in the case of brief quotations embedded in critical reviews or articles.

Cover photo "Roping Up at Camp Muir," Mount Rainier National Park, by Carl Mallery, used with permission.

Disclaimer

Although every effort has been made in the preparation of this book to ensure the accuracy of the information contained therein, this book is provided "as-is" and the publisher, the author(s), their distributors and retailers, as well as all affiliated, related or subsidiary parties take no responsibility for any inaccuracy and any and all damages caused, either directly or indirectly, by the use of such information. We have endeavored to properly provide trademark information on all companies and products mentioned in the book by the appropriate use of capitals. However, we cannot guarantee the accuracy of such information.

musketeers.me, the musketeers.me logo, php[architect], the php[architect] logo are trademarks or registered trademarks of musketeers.me, LLC, its assigns, partners, predecessors and successors. All other trademarks are the property of the respective owners.

Written by
Edward Barnard

Editor
Oscar Merida

Managing Editor
Kara Ferguson

Published by
musketeers.me, LLC.
4627 University Dr
Fairfax, VA 22030 USA

240-348-5PHP (240-348-5747)
info@phparch.com
www.phparch.com

Table of Contents

*To my wife Susan, who has seen me through
40 years of our journey together.*

About the Author

Ed Barnard has experienced two consecutive 20-year careers in software development. He soldered together his first computer from a handful of resistors, diodes, switches, and lights in 1968 at age 10. He taught himself FORTRAN IV two years later. High School brought BASIC. College introduced ALGOL, assembly language, and Pascal.

Funny thing… with ten years of student experience in programming languages, it's the class in assembly-language programming that provided Ed his first 20-year career at Cray Research, "the supercomputing people." He engaged in operating system development in assembly language and C throughout the 1990s on the "biggest" (fastest) hardware of the time. This decade "underneath" the UNIX operating system prepared Ed for his second career.

By the turn of the century, with the World Wide Web ascending, most people coming into the field had strong networking and general IT (Information Technology) experience, but that experience was based on growing up with Windows PCs. Far fewer had production-level UNIX experience. "Just reboot," as with a Windows PC, was not a good answer for production web servers. Ed capitalized on this niche, what we now call DevOps, and rode the tail end of the "dot com boom" into the ground. That foray didn't go well, but began the transition to Perl and PHP scripting languages.

Ed's second 20-year career has been web software development for countless clients, companies, and projects. He enjoys sharing what he's learned along the way through magazine articles, books, and speaking at conferences. Ed and wife Susan have a new hobby—camping the Minnesota winter, allowing them to get back outdoors with no mosquitoes.

Foreword

It's difficult to articulate how excited I was when Ed asked me to write a foreword for *The Fizz Buzz Fix*, and not just because that meant I'd get to read it before it was released (hah!). When Ed and I first met at php[tek] several years ago, we immediately bonded over our shared love for computing history. I started my career in software engineering working on financial systems that ran on hulking, monolithic mainframes. It was the mid-1990s and that technology was already being supplanted by swarms of smaller and much less expensive distributed systems. However, when I look back on those times, I am incredibly grateful that I was able to learn my trade from the generation that came before me.

Though Ed is admittedly a few years older than I am, we had a similar introduction to the industry. We both joined at a young age and had the remarkable privilege of learning at the feet of the previous generation's pioneers. My own start in the industry left me with a powerful and consuming appreciation for the history of computers and the people whose lives have been closely intertwined with them. Friends, coworkers, and fellow conference speakers joke that any time I talk about something, I have to give 40 years of background. That's because I believe that understanding the "why" behind things is every bit as important as the "how."

I caught Ed's talk at php[tek] about Mel, the "Real Programmer," which he references in this book. I was absolutely blown away by how he was able to seamlessly marry a fun story about an irascible programmer sabotaging his company's sales department with a detailed look into how a 60-year-old computer worked, and how the people who programmed it worked. For those of us who've only ever worked in a world with compilers and interpreters and byte-code-chewing virtual machines, the intricacies of a 31-bit drum memory computer are as distant from our day-to-day lives as the Eisenhower administration during which it was built. Yet Ed managed to use that as a backdrop to teach a room full of conference attendees about algorithmic analysis, data encoding, and memory locality. And the room stayed awake!

My education was in biology and—like many people in the classical sciences—I suffer from anxiety and imposter syndrome about computer science topics. Exponential analysis makes way more sense to me in the context of bacterial propagation than the context of nested loops. Somehow, Ed manages to teach these concepts in a way that entirely gets around those anxieties. He brings a level of humor and warmth to these topics that make the complexities behind them seem approachable and even fun.

For one, this book teaches binary algebra from the point of view of a varsity cross country runner. Later, Ed gets into the nuances of producer/consumer architecture through his experiences river rafting. Bridging the practicalities of life with the practicalities of designing and implementing software systems is where Ed is most at home. Each topic he approaches is anchored by a real-world metaphor to help the reader.

Ed instinctively understands that programming is as much art as science. Like a mason, the programmer must understand the science that enables her work. The tensile properties of stone and mortar and the effects of geometry on mass distribution are similar to the time and space efficiencies of an algorithm. But to be a master, the mason must also appreciate the history of the art, and the programmer must do the same.

This book covers deep computer science topics in considerable depth. But don't be intimidated! I found as I read that I was sucked in by Ed's story-telling. One moment I was smiling at the antics of Ed's father's employees. Then, before I knew it, I was detangling the nuances of one's and two's complement and how the Cray supercomputer revolutionized the industry. If you've ever wished you had a deeper understanding of what's happening under the hood of the tools you use as an engineer, and just as importantly, why they work the way they do, this book is a great way to wade in.

I've been incredibly blessed to meet and work with fascinating and brilliant people, both as work colleagues and through my career as a public speaker. Ever since that first time I saw one of Ed's talks, I've had the privilege of being his unofficial cheerleader. He's one of the few conference speakers I consider an absolute must-see, and I am absolutely delighted that people now have the chance to learn from him in an all-new format. Enjoy!

– Samantha Quiñones, 2020

Preface

"Fizz Buzz" is the coding challenge often part of tech interviews. It weeds people out but shouldn't. This book is the first in a series and focuses on teaching the life skills of "learning to learn" and "learning to think like a computer." It's aimed at age 16 and up but is entirely suitable for age 8+.

- Chapter 1: The Fizz Buzz Fix
- Chapter 2: Profile of the "Real Programmer"
- Chapter 3: Think Like a Computer
- Chapter 4: The Basics with a Side of Crypto
- Chapter 5: Design an Algorithm in your Head
- Chapter 6: Abstract Thinking
- Chapter 7: Turtles All The Way Down
- Chapter 8: Deep Dive
- Chapter 9: Impostor Syndrome

About This Book Series

The first book, *The Fizz Buzz Fix: Secrets to Thinking Like an Experienced Software Developer*, directly teaches the skills and thought-processes targeted by those nefarious coding challenges. This book's themes are "learning to learn" and "learn to think like a computer." This is the book I wish I'd read in college or even high school. I wrote this book because I discovered many experts, themselves experienced professionals, missing this background.

The second book is *Mastering Our Craft: A Cray Research Veteran Shares the Secrets*. I continue to encounter people interested—fascinated, actually—in learning about the CRAY-1 supercomputer. Its design, in its innovative simplicity, was groundbreaking in many ways. The facts and figures don't explain its mystique. I was there; I've got the stories and a perspective rarely shared.

Mastering Our Craft leads off with Nathaniel Bowditch, showing how he created so many expert ocean navigators (basically, every ocean navigator by 1840). He simplified and extended the art of navigation, but most importantly, he explained over and over in many different ways. When a sailor reached the "Aha!" moment of understanding, Bowditch wrote down *that* explanation. This series embraces Bowditch's approach.

About This Book

Robert C. Martin, "Uncle Bob," relates to my situation in *Clean Architecture: A Craftsman's Guide to Software Structure and Design* (Prentice Hall, 2018), p. xix:

> *I wrote my very first line of code in 1964, at the age of 12. The year is now 2016, so I have been writing code for more than half a century. In that time, I have learned a few things about how to structure software systems—things that I believe others would likely find valuable.*

I'm running about four years behind Uncle Bob. I soldered together my first computer from a handful of resistors, diodes, switches, and lights in 1968 at age 10. Thus, I too, have passed the half-century mark of playing with computers (as I prefer to think of it, but never tell the boss that).

I was surprised at the extent to which Martin's observations in *Clean Architecture* converge on my own, given that we're writing about two entirely separate topics. Uncle Bob explains what he's learned by reflecting on that half-century of experience (p. xx, emphasis in the original):

> *I've built a lot of apps. I've built a lot of systems. And from them all, and by taking them all into consideration, I've learned something startling.*
>
> **The architecture rules are the same!**
>
> *This is startling because the systems that I have built have been so radically different. Why should such different systems all share similar rules of architecture? My conclusion is* that **the rules of software architecture are independent of every other variable.**

Martin, in his section on designing automated test suites, describes a phenomenon that's far from obvious—and explains my approach to this particular book. *Clean Architecture* p. 252:

> *This separation of evolution is necessary because as time passes, the tests tend to become increasingly more concrete and specific. In contrast, the production code tends to become increasingly more abstract and general. Strong structural coupling prevents—or at least impedes—this necessary evolution, and prevents the production code from being as general, and flexible, as it could be.*

That brings us to this book, *The Fizz Buzz Fix*. What can I share that remains relevant? I've written down the principles, patterns, and approaches that I've seen time and again across the decades. These principles are, as Martin observes about software architecture, "independent of every other variable." They are, from my perspective, timeless. These are the foundations that served me throughout my career.

Like Martin's description of "the production code," you yourself tend to become more abstract and general as you gain experience. We all get better at endeavors through practice. As you gain skill and experience through practice, that experience becomes more abstract. You're able to apply that experience in more and differing situations.

Practicing and demonstrating these skills corresponds to Martin's "the tests." Each time you use (demonstrate) the skill, your demonstration becomes better, more exact, more detailed. You become better at making it look easy. Each practice or demonstration adds to your more-general understanding. It's a feedback loop. It's how we learn.

This, in essence, is the Fizz Buzz challenge. By solving Fizz Buzz, you're demonstrating you understand the underlying principles, patterns, approaches. This demonstration implies that you're able to think like an expert software developer.

The "Fizz Buzz Fix" is remarkably simple—but weird, which makes it remarkably difficult. The weirdness comes from the answer being so abstract. The answer, in my view, is quite literally learning to play with computers. Learn to relate to computers, if you will; learn to see (and, therefore, write) software from the computer's perspective.

Learning to think from a different perspective is not easy—but here we are. Let's do this!

Chapter

1

The Fizz Buzz Fix

As for the snow on top of the mountain a man told me nobody could cross it for a week yet, because he had just done it himself. Was not he a funny man?

–*The Virginian* by Owen Wister (1902)

1. The Fizz Buzz Fix

What's the deal with Fizz Buzz? The Fizz Buzz[1] site outrageously explains:

> *The "Fizz-Buzz test" is an interview question designed to help filter out the 99.5% of programming job candidates who can't seem to program their way out of a wet paper bag.*

That 99.5 percentage comes from the Coding Horror article *Why Can't Programmers… Program?*[2] by Jeff Atwood, co-founder of Stack Overflow[3]:

> *I was incredulous when I read this observation… "Like me, the author is having trouble with the fact that 199 out of 200 applicants for every programming job can't write code at all. I repeat: they can't write any code whatsoever."*
>
> *The author… is evidently turning away lots of programmers who can't write a simple program: "After a fair bit of trial and error I've discovered that people who struggle to code don't just struggle on big problems, or even smallish problems (i.e., write an implementation of a linked list). They struggle with tiny problems."*
>
> **I am disturbed and appalled that any so-called programmer would apply for a job without being able to write the simplest of programs.** *That's a slap in the face to anyone who writes software for a living. (Emphasis in the original.)*

This book is for the 99.5% of us; the 199 out of 200 of us. How do you master the skills expected by Fizz Buzz tests? The answer is a bit weird.

You'll learn that people who have no difficulty with Fizz Buzz think differently and look at things differently. You'll learn those ways of thinking. You'll learn specific skills, but more importantly you'll learn the thought processes and learn to think like an expert software developer.

We know our field is constantly changing. As far back as 1965, Gordon Moore, the co-founder of Fairchild Semiconductor wrote a paper[4] explaining that the number of components per integrated circuit was doubling every year. He expected this trend to continue for at least another decade. A decade later, in 1975, he revised his projection to doubling every two years. This projection, known as Moore's Law, held true through the early 2000s.

---

[1] Fizz Buzz: http://wiki.c2.com/?FizzBuzzTest
[2] Why Can't Programmers… Program?: https://blog.codinghorror.com/why-cant-programmers-program/
[3] Stack Overflow: https://stackoverflow.com
[4] wrote a paper: https://en.wikipedia.org/wiki/Moore%27s_law

Software transforms at a similarly rapid rate, from one year to the next. How do you become an expert in a constantly changing field?

What if you are too young or too old? I've been both. Like "The Virginian" describing a funny man, if somebody can do it, so can you or I.

> *If you think you're beaten, you are;*
> *If you think you dare not, you don't.*
> *If you'd like to win, but you think you can't,*
> *It is almost a cinch you won't.*
>
> *If you think you'll lose, you've lost;*
> *For out in this world we find*
> *Success begins with a person's will*
> *It's all in the state of mind.*
>
> *If you think you're outclassed, you are;*
> *You've got to think high to rise.*
> *You've got to be sure of yourself before*
> *You can ever win the prize.*
>
> *Life's battles don't always go*
> *To the stronger or faster man;*
> *But sooner or later the person who wins*
> *Is the one who thinks he can!*
>
> *—Walter D. Wintle (1905)*

Learn From the Enemy

This book came quite by accident. I wanted to write about computing history. I knew it was boring, but I was convinced it was important, so I went ahead and wrote it down. I discovered something! I discovered I can teach you how to think like an expert software developer, right now, regardless of your age.

To understand, I need to tell you my story of accidentally following the clues.

I was part of a small software development team in 2015. The company's web site came under attack by hackers using an approach we hadn't seen before. I designed a new security system and was pleased with the result. This was the first step; I had no idea where it would lead the next few years.

Figure 1.1. First conference presentation

I thought this might be a good topic for php[architect] magazine. I wrote up a possible article and sent it, unsolicited, to the editor. I never heard back and didn't worry about it. I had fun writing the 30 pages and it served as a good feature design documentation for the company; I figured that was good enough.

A few months later I happened to attend my second software developers' conference, php[tek]. There was a php[architect] vendor table, and I asked about the article. It turned out my submission was trapped in a spam folder and never seen. It was immediately accepted to be published, and *Learn From the Enemy*[5] was in the May 2016 issue.

I explained my best advice concerning website security comes from *Ender's Game* by Orson Scott Card (the book, not the horrible movie adaptation):

> *You will be about to lose, Ender, but you will win. You will learn to defeat the enemy. He will teach you how.*

This had nothing to do with the "Fizz Buzz Fix"…yet. But it set me on the path to discovering the fix. "Fizz Buzz" itself will teach us how.

At that software developers' conference, the conference speakers encouraged others to become speakers as well. We've all solved problems, learned things. When people share their hard-won knowledge, everyone wins. I found there was even a group of mentors available[6] for helping to craft conference-talk proposals.

---

[5] *Learn From the Enemy:* <u>https://phpa.me/learn-from-enemy-may16</u>
[6] *group of mentors available:* <u>https://helpmeabstract.com</u>

I worked with the mentors to craft various proposals based on "Learn From the Enemy." My "Using Encryption in PHP" proposal did get picked (Figure 1.1). But the next step on our path was an unrelated remark. I explained I had never given a conference talk, but that I "used to teach Cray supercomputer operating system internals (assembly and octal) as Senior Instructor for Cray Research Software Training."

My mentor ended the feedback with, "The Cray experience you mention off-hand sounds like a talk or two in its own right… lessons from the first supercomputers or something, applying the engineering concepts you used there to pretty much whatever topic you'd like to speak on!"

I followed that advice. I showed what it was like programming the CRAY-1, and shared some of the mystique. People loved it! But over time I got unexpected feedback.

People whom I know to be highly knowledgeable software developers themselves said the Cray talk passed over their heads. There was a knowledge gap; a missing skill I had assumed everyone had. It's a simple skill—binary arithmetic[7]. It was a skill I'd learned in grade school.

I asked the local high school's math teachers. Do they teach binary arithmetic, radix conversion, anything like that, to anyone, at any level? No, they don't. Not in any primary or secondary grade level, and not in any "advanced placement" class either. My own college courses in the 1970s assumed students already had this skill; however, modern Computer Science courses do not appear to include these skills.

I began teaching binary arithmetic myself. It's a skill that I've used throughout my career; I, therefore, assumed it would be important for everyone else. It isn't, but this was the next step along my trail of clues.

I reached a weird impasse in my own mind. I had remained convinced, for four decades and more at this point, that the "binary skills" are important and relevant. Never mind that almost nobody else saw things this way. This weird attitude becomes the key to the puzzle. We don't even know what the puzzle is yet, but we do have a key waiting to be used.

In 2019, I helped design a three-day curriculum for teaching *Professional PHP* at php[tek]. I immediately "called dibs" on the binary stuff. That's the part I enjoy teaching the most! But most professional software developers don't do bit manipulation or binary arithmetic in their day-to-day lives. So we left the irrelevant "binary stuff" out of the curriculum.

I decided to write everything down. That would allow me to get it off my mind and move on. I could then focus on the *Professional PHP* curriculum we were developing. I began that obscure book by discussing the test called "Fizz Buzz," which we often encounter in

_____

[7]   binary arithmetic: *https://www.cs.nmsu.edu/~hdp/cs273/notes/binary.html*

job interviews for software-development positions. Sure enough, I wrote the "Fizz Buzz Fix" right into that book (which became this book you're now reading) without realizing it!

We began this trail with *Learn From the Enemy* and discovered that Fizz Buzz is the enemy. The idea that "99.5% of programming job candidates can't seem to program their way out of a wet paper bag" has become common wisdom in many circles—especially in those circles hiring software developers like you and I. We'll see how harmful this "common wisdom" is in Chapter 2; Fizz Buzz explicitly selects against diversity in the workforce.

This claim, that only 0.5% of candidates can pass the Fizz Buzz test, becomes the next point on our trail of clues. I am, quite by accident, one of those "0.5%" people.

I originally wrote the book, without realizing it, for that 0.5%. I did not explain why I wrote any specific chapter of the book. I thought the reason would be self-evident; and, perhaps it would be to that 0.5%.

There's an old story of a Professor of Mathematics giving a lecture to her class. This was a large lecture hall with a chalkboard at the front. She'd written out a mathematical theorem on the board. She began the lecture by explaining the theorem. She said its proof was self-evident.

Then she stopped.

She turned to the board, her back to the audience. She stood there. She seemed to be pondering the theorem. She stood there pondering for a full fifteen minutes.

She finally turned back to the class full of confidence. She stated, "Yes. The proof is self-evident," and continued with her lecture.

I'm no professor of mathematics, but I have the same difficulty here. To me, it's self-evident as to *why* a specific chapter is important and relevant. But it's not evident to anyone else! There's a difference in the way of thinking.

The people who think about things a certain way have no difficulty with "Fizz Buzz" tests. I know from associating with these people over the decades that we actually do look at things differently when it comes to software and computers. With each chapter, we'll be explaining and teaching that thinking. That's the "Fizz Buzz Fix."

The Skills

Parisa Tabriz[8]'s official title, as of when she wrote *So you want to work in security?*[9], was *Security Princess* at Google. She's often asked how to get into the field. She explains:

---

[8]   *Parisa Tabriz:* https://twitter.com/laparisa
[9]   *So you want to work in security?:* https://phpa.me/want-work-security

> *If I've learned anything, I've learned that there is no single, standard, or best preparatory path.*
>
> *Independent of how you acquire it, you'll benefit from having a strong understanding of applied computer science, or how computers and software work. Much of applied computer science is about solving problems with layers of abstraction, and security is often about finding the flawed assumptions in those abstractions... and then figuring out how to best fix (or exploit) them.*

Software development is based on obscure fundamentals such as binary arithmetic. We know these skills are not generally taught in school. How, then, are we to learn? We'll learn right here.

We'll learn to think like a computer. We'll learn about binary number representation, both ones' complement and two's complement notation. We'll see truth tables and Boolean expressions. That can get pretty boring. But then being able to pass coding interviews with ease? I hope you find that as cool as I do. Think of it as an achievement unlocked!

Having survived those fundamentals, we'll make a fun foray into algorithm design. Fun? Yes! You'll learn to do things in your head, without computers or calculators, that you didn't realize you could do. That will be another achievement unlocked.

By this point, we'll have learned some probably-new skills. But the question is, does anyone use these skills in the 21st Century? Certainly. That's why we're here.

We'll extend our newly-won skills by taking a deep dive inside the PHP compiler. This won't be comprehensive. We'll focus on one specific area, namely how PHP arrays are implemented. If you want to dive further into the PHP internals on your own, you'll now be prepared to do so. By digging into *one* area in-depth, we've prepared ourselves to take on *any* area in depth.

Is this deep dive relevant only to PHP programmers or compiler writers? Certainly not! The skill to learn, here, is the ability to take a deep dive into any complex system. I would take a similar approach when trying to learn any large open-source project, for example, in any programming language.

Our upcoming foray begins with the premise that 99.5% of programming job candidates can't seem to program their way out of a wet paper bag. That's bogus and we'll see why. We'll also see this as a strong indication our current system is broken.

Our final chapter talks about Impostor Syndrome. Anyone can become *an* expert, but I found Imposter Syndrome requires me to be **the one foremost** expert, or it doesn't count.

I'm not that foremost expert and never have been. This and other issues of mental wellness affect a large proportion of our industry. We'll see ways to move forward.

What Is the Fizz Buzz Fix?

What exactly is "The Fizz Buzz Fix?" It's not about cheating on the "Fizz Buzz" test. We'll complete Fizz Buzz in the next section, but we're here for far more than that specific test.

We're here to master a skill. Those who have mastered this skill won't have any difficulty with small coding challenges like Fizz Buzz. I call this skill "learning to learn."

Bruce Lee, possibly the greatest martial artist in living memory, stated, "Be like water, my friend." Water instantly adapts to its environment.

Lee, quoted in *The Warrior Within: The Philosophies of Bruce Lee*[10] by John Little, describes his own self-expression:

> *Jeet kune do is training and discipline toward the ultimate reality of combat. The ultimate reality is simple, direct, and free. A true jeet kune do man never opposes force or gives way completely. He is pliable as a spring and complements his opponent's strength. He uses his opponent's technique to create his own. You should respond to any circumstance without prearrangement; your action should be as fast as a shadow adapting to a moving object.*

Bruce's son Brandon Lee explains in the same book,

> *[The master] always talks about teaching "jeet kune do concepts." In other words, teaching someone the concepts, a certain way of thinking about the martial arts, as opposed to teaching them techniques. To me, that kind of illustrates the difference between giving someone a fish and teaching them how to fish. You could teach someone a certain block, and then they have that certain block; or you can teach someone the concept behind such a block, and then you have given them an entire area of thinking that they can grow and evolve in themselves. They can say: "Oh, I see—if that's the concept, then you could probably also perform it this way or that way and still remain true to the concept."*

---

[10] *The Warrior Within: The Philosophies of Bruce Lee*: https://amazon.com/dp/0809231948

Consider Brandon Lee's explanation the other way around. We can't learn the theory behind that certain block without first learning the block. Furthermore, we need to learn that specific block *well* before considering the underlying theory.

The "Fizz Buzz Fix" is, literally, learning to learn. We'll be learning specific skills related to software development. We'll also be learning *why* we're learning each specific skill; that is, we'll be learning "the concept behind the block"—but only after we've learned the block.

The Fizz Buzz test aims to identify those relatively rare people who *can* program their way out of a wet paper bag. There's a "way of thinking" involved. I call it an "affinity for computers." For anyone who's had an unsuccessful encounter with Fizz Buzz, we'll be fixing *that* problem once and for all.

The Fizz Buzz Test

The Fizz Buzz Test[11] assignment is:

> *Write a program that prints the numbers from 1 to 100. But for multiples of three print "Fizz" instead of the number and for the multiples of five print "Buzz." For numbers which are multiples of both three and five print "FizzBuzz."*

This originally was a children's game aimed at helping students learn division skills. The teacher would point to each student in turn, counting from one to some maximum number. The key numbers might be five and seven, for example, if those were the multiplication/division skills being taught that day.

Listing 1.1 is my solution when asked to implement Fizz Buzz in PHP. It stops at 20 rather than 100 to reduce output volume.

---

[11] *Fizz Buzz Test:* https://wiki.c2.com/?FizzBuzzTest

1. The Fizz Buzz Fix

Listing 1.1

```php
1. <?php
2. declare(strict_types=1);
3.
4. $i = 0;
5. while (++$i < 21) {
6.     if (!($i % 15)) {
7.         echo "FizzBuzz";
8.     } elseif (!($i % 5)) {
9.         echo "Buzz";
10.    } elseif (!($i % 3)) {
11.        echo "Fizz";
12.    } else {
13.        echo $i;
14.    }
15.    echo PHP_EOL;
16. }
17.
18. echo "Task complete." . PHP_EOL;
```

The output is:

Output 1.1

```
1
2
Fizz
4
Buzz
Fizz
7
8
Fizz
Buzz
11
Fizz
13
14
FizzBuzz
16
17
Fizz
19
Buzz
Task complete.
```

Why did I structure the code as I did? Certainly many different solutions are correct.

- Line 4: With a single simple loop, it's often clearest to use $i as the increment variable. That's actually a hold-over from the earliest days of Fortran programming, where the letter I had a specific meaning as a variable name. That fact is not relevant here unless I'm in an actual job interview and my interviewer is impressed by such things.

- Line 5: With a simple loop like here, I prefer to increment the loop variable inside the loop-control part. It's easy to forget to increment the variable if it's supposed to get incremented somewhere inside the loop. A for loop would have worked just as well here, but I see while more commonly than for in PHP, so I prefer to use the more-familiar construct.

- Line 6: The instruction "multiples of three and five" means "divisible by 15." Thus, to get the words right, we need to first check for being divisible by 15, then by five, then by three. Since I'm writing the if/elseif blocks in reverse order from the instructions, I double-checked to make sure "buzz" is for five and "fizz" is for three.

- Line 6, continued: The % operator indicates modulo arithmetic. If a number modulo 15 is zero, that means it's divisible by 15. Conversely, if a number modulo 15 is not zero, that means it's not divisible by 15. In PHP, zero or not-zero becomes false or true here, and the NOT operator ! reverses the answer, becoming true or false. Thus, this test reads as "is divisible by 15". At line 8 and line 10 we have "is divisible by 5" and "is divisible by 3" respectively.

For the record, this solution could be expressed in exactly half as many lines of code, producing the identical result:

Listing 1.2

```
 1. <?php
 2.
 3. $i = 0;
 4. while (++$i < 21) {
 5.     if      (!($i % 15)) echo "FizzBuzz\n";
 6.     elseif (!($i % 5))  echo "Buzz\n";
 7.     elseif (!($i % 3))  echo "Fizz\n";
 8.     else                echo "$i\n";
 9. }
10. echo "Task complete.\n";
```

However, in modern software development, reducing the lines of code is rarely the point. Code that's more readable, more maintainable, more comprehensible, will generally be superior code—no matter the programming language.

Chapter

2

Profile of the "Real Programmer"

The tech interview process is badly broken in a way that helps drive women and all kinds of minorities out of our industry. We'll look at the coding challenges we see during the modern tech interview. We step back in time to learn about the so-called "Real Programmer" to discover the "Real Programmer" is the same type of person selected by modern-day coding challenges. We need to first understand and recognize the "Real Programmer" so we can learn from them.

Coding Challenges

Let's begin with an aspect of modern life in high technology—the tech interview that includes a coding challenge. This seems reasonable on the surface, but I believe it's a key component of the badly broken system that's driving women and people of color out of our industry.

That's a strong statement. To clearly see what I mean, we need to visit several topics; let's start with the coding challenge.

I've encountered several such coding challenges for job interviews. In each case, the company or recruiter said people had trouble with these. That seemed strange because I did *not* have trouble. In one case, the interviewers were surprised by how quickly I finished the challenge; in another case, no one had yet passed the challenge. This was *not* because I'm a better candidate or some such nonsense. What's really going on here?

None of these challenges had anything to do with designing a web application, even though most people in my field do just that. Nor do we generally start from scratch. There's usually an existing codebase and a problem to be solved—that's why we are having this interview. But these challenges have nothing to do with the reason I'm being interviewed. That's weird. Why did the interviewers ask this question? In fact, a pattern emerges.

Online searches confirm the intent—there's a dark side breaking our industry. Sure enough, this type of interview challenge is called *Fizz Buzz*, and it's based on the surprising premise that most computer science graduates, and most professional software developers, "can't seem to program their way out of a wet paper bag."

We'll first review the reason Fizz Buzz was created. Then, we'll take a step back in time, to 1982, and encounter the famous *Real Programmers Don't Use Pascal*. We'll bring those two themes together to see what's broken.

Fizz Buzz

Each of the challenges I encountered was of the form "write the code to make these tests pass." Each included a clear statement of the problem and instructions for running the tests. None of these challenges had anything to do with building web pages.

That is certainly strange. Why bother with a coding challenge which has nothing to do with the actual job requirements?

Are these Kobayashi Maru[1] scenarios, that is, no-win situations? Yes, and no. One objective of the coding challenge is to observe how you perform during the scenario. It can be a win-win situation rather than a no-win situation.

You will recall from the first chapter that the Fizz Buzz[2] site explains:

> The "Fizz-Buzz test" is an interview question designed to help filter out the 99.5% of programming job candidates who can't seem to program their way out of a wet paper bag.

You will also recall this 99.5 percentage comes from the Coding Horror article *Why Can't Programmers… Program?*[3] by Jeff Atwood.

Both articles are worth reading in their entirety (and they're short). The Coding Horror comments section debates the merits of Fizz Buzz-style questions, e.g., does not being able to implement recursion mean you're not a good programmer? I'll show my snarky recursion solution in the next section.

Coding Horror explains why interviewers are presenting these sorts of challenges—again, people "can't seem to program their way out of a wet paper bag."

This claim is both harsh and unfair. If 99.5% of job candidates have trouble with these coding challenges, that tells us either:

- These coding challenges have nothing to do with, and are irrelevant as, predictors of actual job performance; or
- Our training system has nothing to do with, and has no relevance to, our real-world jobs; or
- Both of the above.

The problem, as we'll see, is more subtle. We're selecting *against* diversity while *appearing* fair and transparent.

Our next step is to examine Fizz Buzz's explicitly evil cousin, a specific type of whiteboard interview. But first, let's have some fun with my solution to "can you do recursion?"

---

[1]   Kobayashi Maru: https://en.wikipedia.org/wiki/Kobayashi_Maru
[2]   Fizz Buzz: http://wiki.c2.com/?FizzBuzzTest
[3]   Why Can't Programmers… Program?: https://blog.codinghorror.com/why-cant-programmers-program/

Figure 2.1. Meta Data

Recursion

During September 2010 I was driving through the Ozark Mountains in Missouri and discovered the town of Meta. I definitely wasn't lost; I was merely enjoying unexpected scenery. I turned around and returned to the edge of town to take the photo in Figure 2.1.

The sign was helpful! It inspired me to stop and take this metadata photo, which in turn, inspired me to get out the map and discover where I wasn't. I was supposed to take a left turn ten miles back.

The sign's interesting because we use "metadata" constantly in modern software development. Metadata is information about something that's kept separate, not a part of the thing. We see this a lot with websites, databases, and so on.

As another example, digital photos include "exif" data. That includes the date and time the photo was taken, (often) where the photo was taken, and what type of camera took the photo. This information is a form of metadata.

One of the more ridiculous interview challenges is "implement this algorithm using recursion." The interviewer doesn't care if you can write good software; if you can't implement recursion, their company won't be needing you. It doesn't matter that very few software developers actually use recursion in their day-to-day jobs.

> *Recursion[4] occurs when a thing is defined in terms of itself or of its type. Recursion is used in a variety of disciplines ranging from linguistics to logic. The most common application of recursion is in mathematics and computer science, where a function being defined is applied within its own definition. While this apparently defines an infinite number of instances (function values), it is often done in such a way that no loop or infinite chain of references can occur.*

This sign carries information about the town of Meta, Missouri, while standing outside of, and therefore separate from, Meta. This sign, by definition, is metadata consisting of Meta data, which is totally meta.

Whiteboard Interview

The "Fizz Buzz" test has an explicitly evil cousin, a certain type of whiteboard interview. Let's take a look.

Adrianne Jeffries in *Programmers are confessing their coding sins to protest a broken job interview process*[5] shows how a particular form of whiteboard interview selects *against* a diverse population.

> *This interview style, widely used by major tech companies including Google and Amazon, typically pits candidates against a whiteboard without access to reference material—a scenario working programmers say is demoralizing and an unrealistic test of actual ability.*

David Heinemeier Hansson[6], the creator of Ruby on Rails, describes the process as "whiteboard algorithm hazing."

Max Howell[7] adds, "Google: 90% of our engineers use the software you wrote (Homebrew), but you can't invert a binary tree on a whiteboard so f— off." Someone else in that discussion mentioned they regularly look up material in books *they wrote*.

How does this elitist whiteboard hazing work against people? It selects for recent college graduates who have studied-up on those algorithms. It works against people with real-world experience who have been writing software for a decade or four. It also works against people

---

[4] Recursion: https://en.wikipedia.org/wiki/Recursion

[5] Programmers are confessing their coding sins to protest a broken job interview process: https://phpa.me/protest-broken-interview

[6] David Heinemeier Hansson: https://twitter.com/dhh/status/834146806594433025

[7] Max Howell: https://twitter.com/mxcl/status/608682016205344768

who didn't receive a very-costly education, including working against graduates of coding boot camps. It works against people who are already employed full time, or have other full time responsibilities, with little extra time to study-up on whiteboard answers.

At best, the perpetrators of this system are implicitly selecting for people just like themselves.

Aline Lerner, in *You can't fix diversity in tech without fixing the technical interview*[8] presents charts showing ways this process adversely impacts diverse groups. She explains the process, statistically, proves to be non-deterministic. Interviewees can't tell how they did; results are arbitrary. Impostor Syndrome kicks in, and those susceptible stop interviewing altogether.

> *At the end of the day, because technical interviewing is indeed a game, like all games, it takes practice to improve. However, unless you've been socialized to expect and prepare for the game-like aspect of the experience, it's not something that you can necessarily intuit.*
>
> *Also, if you go into your interviews expecting them to be indicative of your aptitude at the job, which is, at the outset, not an unreasonable assumption, you will be crushed the first time you crash and burn. But the process isn't a great or predictable indicator of your aptitude. On top of that, you likely can't tell how you're doing even when you do well.*

Lerner also explains the origin of puzzles in software developer interviews. Fortunately, I've not seen such puzzles lately, but ten years ago I was passed a wood-and-string puzzle during an interview. We continued talking. I soon passed it back, taken apart (i.e., solved). The interview team was surprised and said none of their other candidates had solved it. I didn't mention I'd seen and solved it before.

This broken interview process doesn't serve the employer well either. We have a concrete well-established process for selecting people who can solve a specific puzzle. We don't seem to have any such process for the more important skills such as communicating with other people or dealing with unexpected situations, let alone designing for those unexpected situations.

There's a pattern here, and it's nefarious. But to identify that pattern we must first step back in time to 1982.

---

[8]   *You can't fix diversity in tech without fixing the technical interview*: https://phpa.me/fix-diversity-tech

Insecurities

Home computers appeared in the 1970s. By 1982, Radio Shack had sold over 100,000 of their TRS-80 home computer. Apple worked with MECC[9], the Minnesota Educational Computing Consortium, to get Apple computers placed in public schools. The plan worked. You may recall some of the beloved MECC titles like Oregon Trail[10].

This advent of the TRS-80 (Figure 2.2), Apple II, Commodore, Atari, and other home computers, transformed our view of our own profession in that this caused fear—fundamental endemic fear—for our jobs, our livelihood. The job fears were real because this was the first generation of children with access to computers. Computer programming had now been a profession for three or four decades. Now, teenagers potentially had equal footing with adults in the job market.

Figure 2.3 shows my son Jakob with his first home computer the Apple][+. Purchase price, with additional hardware and software add-ons, was around $2,100 (price in 2019 would be $8,859.40). He didn't yet know how to type, so I took care of it for him for several years. The monitor is to the right of the keyboard. The floppy disk drive is atop the main unit containing motherboard, extension cards, and keyboard. The gray plastic file box on its left was storage for the 5-1/4" floppy disks. There's a box of spare floppy disks (for backups) to the right of the monitor. That's a Cray Assembly Language coding form underneath the Cray Research coffee mug. I'd been using coding forms to write out the code long-hand for more than 12 years by this point, so using the pre-printed form was second nature. The gold USAF Academy bathrobe came in handy during our first Minnesota winter!

This may sound ridiculous to the modern ear because many of us have heard questions like "Why should I pay you to build webpages when my 12-year-old could do it?" But in 1982 computer programmers, to this point, were much like rocket scientists. Neither was a profession one could easily learn in high school. Rocket scientists required the resources to design and build towering rockets. Computer programmers depended on entire rooms full of computing equipment.

Meanwhile, the U.S. Constitution's proposed Equal Rights Amendment[11] was nearly ratified by its original 1979 deadline, receiving 35 of the needed 38 state ratifications. Then, Phyllis Schlafly[12] (in my opinion) single-handedly defeated the ratification. The activism and upheaval became part of an ongoing battle, "the battle of the sexes," which took its name

---

[9]   MECC: https://en.wikipedia.org/wiki/MECC
[10] Oregon Trail: https://phpa.me/wikip-oregon-trail
[11] Equal Rights Amendment: https://en.wikipedia.org/wiki/Equal_Rights_Amendment
[12] Phyllis Schlafly: https://en.wikipedia.org/wiki/Phyllis_Schlafly

Figure 2.2. TRS-80 Model 4

Figure 2.3. Apple II+, late 1982

from the highly-publicized exhibition tennis match[13] between Billie Jean King and Bobby Riggs in 1973.

Why do we care? Because these events converged on the lackluster book *Real Men Don't Eat Quiche: A Guidebook to All That is Truly Masculine*[14], a best-seller throughout the summer of 1982. This book poked fun at the concept of "Real Men," contrasting them to men getting more out of life, the "quiche eaters."

> *Quiche eater: "A man who is a dilettante, a trend-chaser, an over-anxious conformist, one who eschews (or merely lacks) the traditional masculine virtues.*

Let me be clear here, lest we miss the context a generation later: The book is a *JOKE*. A satire. A way of poking fun at real insecurities faced by our society at the time.

Ed Post of Tektronix continued the "quiche eater" joke. He changed the phrase from "Real Men" to "Real Programmers" and spun an over-the-top tale in honor of computer programmers, *Real Programmers Don't Use Pascal*[15]. This story entered the annals of "hacker folklore" wherein the hero accomplished feats not to be expected from mere mortals.

Post's underlying message was that "real" computer programmers should not be replaced by the younger generation. He begins, as they all do, by talking of the "good old days" which were really never that good:

> *Back in the good old days, the "Golden Era" of computers, it was easy to separate the adults from the children, sometimes called "Real Men" and "Quiche Eaters" in the literature… During this period, the Real Programmers were the ones who understood computer programming, and the Quiche Eaters were the ones who didn't. The Real Programmer is in danger of becoming extinct, being replaced by high-school students playing Pac-Man with TRASH-80s!*

Did you catch the connection? The "Real Programmer" is exactly the person who could handle the "Fizz Buzz" challenge. Fizz Buzz, and the whiteboard interview, explicitly selects for Real Programmers who "understand computer programming."

---

[13] *exhibition tennis match:* https://en.wikipedia.org/wiki/Battle_of_the_Sexes_(tennis
[14] *Real Men Don't Eat Quiche: A Guidebook to All That is Truly Masculine:*
     https://en.wikipedia.org/wiki/Real_Men_Don%27t_Eat_Quiche
[15] *Real Programmers Don't Use Pascal:* https://en.wikipedia.org/wiki/Real_Programmers_Don%27t_Use_Pascal

2. Profile of the "Real Programmer"

Post sounds the alarm:

> *There is a clear need to point out these differences: Help employers of Real Program-mers to realize why it would be a mistake to replace the Real Programmers on their staff with 12-year-old Pac-Man players (at a considerable salary savings).*

Post then enumerates our differences, giving voice to our fears.

> *The easiest way to tell a Real Programmer from the crowd is by the programming language he or she uses. Real Programmers use FORTRAN. Quiche Eaters use PASCAL. Real Programmers actually talked in capital letters, you understand.*
>
> *Niklaus Wirth, the designer of PASCAL, was asked, "How do you pronounce your name?"*
>
> *He replied, "You can either call me by name, pronouncing it 'Veert,' or call me by value, 'Worth.'" One can tell immediately from this comment that Niklaus Wirth is a Quiche Eater.*

In other words, Real Programmers are Serious, and don't do cute. To fully appreciate the joke, you need to know that one of the differences "under the covers" between FORTRAN and PASCAL was "call by name" versus "call by value."

Wirth was making a joke about a joke. You won't be surprised, therefore, to learn Wirth's comment has itself made it into the annals of hacker folklore. Nowadays we could change PASCAL to PHP and change FORTRAN to JAVA with similar effect.

There's an elitist irony here regarding COBOL. COBOL (an acronym for Common Business Oriented Language) was the business language of choice well into the 1980s. Because most large mainframes were purchased for business use, COBOL had by far the largest market share of all "higher level" programming languages. But COBOL programming wasn't "cool" like FORTRAN. Nor was it "cool" like the object-oriented languages appearing from the 1990s onward. But, funny thing, there likely are still more lines of COBOL running in production in 2020 than all "cooler" languages combined!

Pascal arrived in 1974 as the weirdly-titled book *PASCAL User Manual and Report*[16]. Once again, context is everything. The weird title is a nod to the programming language Algol. All modern C-like programming languages derive from Algol. Algol-58 was described in the 1958 *Preliminary report*, and Algol-60 by the *Revised Report on the Algorithmic Language Algol 60*.

---

[16] *PASCAL User Manual and Report*: https://dl.acm.org/citation.cfm?id=574137

The Pascal book's original title points out another weirdness of the time. FORTRAN (Formula Translation), COBOL (Common Business-Oriented Language), BASIC (Beginner's All-Purpose Symbolic Instruction Code), and ALGOL (Algorithmic Language) were all acronyms and therefore written with upper-case letters. Pascal, for whatever reason, was introduced as PASCAL. Programmers really did talk in capital letters back then!

Wirth's own evolution of Algol-60, which he called Algol-W, was declined by the Algol-68 committee in favor of a more complex language. Wirth moved on to develop Pascal, announcing it with a nod to the "real" Algol (by using the word "Report" in the book title). Such are the politics of computer science.

Pascal thus arrived just in time to be adopted by quiche-eating Computer Science departments and laughed-at by Real Programmers standing fearfully next to their TRASH-80s.

Post's essay disparaged the then-modern theory behind Computer Science:

> *Real Programmers don't need abstract concepts to get their jobs done. They are perfectly happy with a keypunch, a FORTRAN IV compiler, and some pizza. If you can't do it in FORTRAN, do it in assembly language. If you can't do it in assembly language, it isn't worth doing.*

This was 1982. We at Cray Research were delighted with Post's declaration:

> *Legend has it that Seymour Cray, inventor of the CRAY-1 supercomputer and most of Control Data's computers, actually toggled the first operating system for the CDC 7600 in on the front panel from memory when it was first powered on. Seymour, needless to say, is a Real Programmer.*

While I don't personally know if that particular "Seymour Story" is true or not, it's certainly plausible. Back then it would have been unremarkable. Seymour Cray, as a computer designer since the 1950s, would have been entering boot programs through the front panel for more than a decade at that point. Not being able to program and boot his own computer, unaided, *would* have been remarkable.

Post's essay is brilliant, describing the many characteristics and situations of our heroic computer programmer. We learn:

> *The Real Programmer is capable of working 30, 40, even 50 hours at a stretch, under intense pressure. In fact, he prefers it that way... If there is not enough schedule pressure on the Real Programmer, he tends to make things more challenging by working on one small*

> but interesting part of the problem for the first nine weeks, then finishing the rest in the last week, in two or three 50-hour marathons. This not only impresses the hell out of his manager, who was despairing of ever getting the project done on time, but creates a convenient excuse for not doing the documentation.
>
> A real programmer might or might not know his wife's name. He does, however, know the entire ASCII (or EBCDIC) code table.

This attitude remains true but harmful. Eugene Kim's article *Yahoo CEO Marissa Mayer explains how she worked 130 hours a week and why it matters*[17]:

> She's regularly pulled off all-nighters during her time at Google, and even worked from her hospital bed shortly after having her twins last year… Mayer says hard work is an important part of any business and an often overlooked part of Google's success.
>
> "Could you work 130 hours in a week?" The answer is yes, if you're strategic about when you sleep, when you shower, and how often you go to the bathroom. The nap rooms at Google were there because it was safer to stay in the office than walk to your car at 3 a.m. For my first five years, I did at least one all-nighter a week, except when I was on vacation—and the vacations were few and far between.
>
> Being there on the weekend is a huge indicator of success, mostly because these companies don't just happen. They happen because of really hard work.

There's a pattern here. We are *not* selecting for work/life balance, or a diverse workforce. Whether unintentionally or not, we are actually selecting for mental health problems, burnout, and higher rates of project failure. As we saw in *Real Programmers Don't Use Pascal*, this pattern began at least half a century ago.

Meanwhile, what *are* Fizz Buzz, whiteboard hazing, and heroic folklore all selecting for? I have a theory—and I fit the profile.

Profile Describing a Real Programmer

Different people think differently. The Myers-Briggs Type Indicator[18] attempts to standardize this observation, claiming that people falling into the same category (there are 16 categories) have some characteristics in common.

---

[17] *Yahoo CEO Marissa Mayer explains how she worked 130 hours a week and why it matters:*
   https://phpa.me/yahoo-mayer-130
[18] *Myers-Briggs Type Indicator:* https://phpa.me/mbti-basics

The MBTI is not considered as authoritative or accepted as it once was. Our point here is to note that different people think differently and that some people do have similar characteristics. It's often true that "birds of a feather flock together."

Suppose that Fizz Buzz—whether intentionally or not—precisely selects for a very specific profile. Suppose it's not selecting the "best" 0.5% of the general population, as intended, but is instead selecting members of a very specific population. It's no coincidence that this selected population displays the same characteristics described as a Real Programmer.

For example, I've asked a few people I know who identify as INTJ on the Myers-Briggs scale. I asked if they are good at identifying patterns. The answer has always been yes. It's a small sample size, fewer than a dozen people, but I find the result interesting because I too recognize patterns others don't. It's a useful skill in the hard sciences, including hard-core Real Programming.

From what I can remember of the Stanford-Binet evaluations (the "IQ test"), it too selected for these same sorts of characteristics. I only vaguely recall a few wisps after 50 years, but remember that one of the sections was to be verbally told a string of digits, and I was to repeat them back in reverse order, with the strings of digits becoming longer and longer.

That's the sort of trick that comes naturally to a Real Programmer whereas other more normal tests are outside a Real Programmer's comprehension or interest.

As another example, I've been telling people for years that it's really important to understand how computers and software work. I have *always* taken advantage of *my* knowledge in that area. So I have blithely assumed anyone else in our profession with similar knowledge would *also* use that knowledge to advantage.

Post's essay shares a similar assumption:

> *What of the future? It is a matter of some concern to Real Programmers that the latest generation of computer programmers are not being brought up with the same outlook on life as their elders. Many of them have never seen a computer with a front panel. Hardly anyone graduating from school these days can do hex arithmetic without a calculator.*

Decades later, it does appear the software industry has survived—even though it remains true that hardly anyone graduating from school these days can do hex arithmetic without a calculator.

I interpret the Fizz Buzz premise to mean that 99.5% of current software developers do not match the "Real Programmer" profile. Post's essay, in effect, proclaims the Real Programmer is a rare phenomenon. The Jargon File 4.4.7[19] notes:

> A Real Programmer's code can awe with its fiendish brilliance, even as its crockishness appalls… and terrify the crap out of other programmers—because someday, somebody else might have to try to understand their code in order to change it. Their successors generally consider it a Good Thing that there aren't many Real Programmers around any more.

Modern tech interviews are seeking Real Programmers whether they realize it or not. They're simply interviewing "the way it's always been done" without realizing the horrific premise behind Fizz Buzz. The interviews are, therefore, excluding most of humanity, and that particularly means excluding anyone with a life outside of work. Schools, even down to kindergarten and earlier, are pushing for computer-programming literacy, yet we continue to select only for Real Programmers. Our selection process is definitely working against our own best interests.

This is why the interviewers are consistently surprised when they *do* encounter someone fitting that profile. That person may or may not be a useful employee once hired, but it's an easy guarantee that he or she can do Fizz Buzz variations all day long, in octal or hexadecimal.

Track and Field

I don't want to give the impression that anyone can become an expert, or master a skill by merely reading a book. Mastery requires work—and determination. It often requires a mentor and an accountability partner.

My senior year in high school was my fourth year on the high school cross country team. I was so bad that I received the "most improved runner" award *twice* during those four years. Steve, the other senior on the cross country team that fall, was the team captain.

Figure 2.4 shows Steve and I during the mile run during Track season in the spring. Our uniforms included white socks with the team colors, green and gold.

Colleen, now starting her junior year in high school, had performed exceptionally well during the spring track-and-field season. Those boys who ran cross country in the fall usually also competed on the track team in the spring. Girls had no such option; girls had no cross country team, only track.

---

[19] The Jargon File 4.4.7: http://www.catb.org/jargon/html/R/Real-Programmer.html

Figure 2.4. Ed, center left with Steve in front, center right

Figure 2.5. Timberline High School Cross Country team, late 1974

Colleen received permission to join the cross country team as the only girl, competing amongst the boys. Each of the high schools had a varsity squad and a junior varsity (JV) squad. Varsity competed against varsity, and JV competed against JV, at the various meets.

The Varsity rule was quite simple. If you could keep up, you ran varsity. If you choked, you ran JV and somebody else got to take your spot. Colleen ran exclusively JV, so there was no concern about her taking one of the coveted varsity spots.

Figure 2.5 shows Colleen at front center. I'm at the back left next to Coach Bykerk. Steve is at back right. The bright yellow jackets indicate the varsity team and they were numbered 1 through 7. I wore 3 that week and Steve wore 4, but it was usually the other way around. The dark green uniforms were the JV. Normal team size was about double what's in this photo.

Colleen, to the best of my recollection, was not there to break barriers. She was there to train in the offseason. Her focus was on the half-mile and mile events during Track season in the spring. It was pointless for her to train with other girls; they literally could not keep up. Only the boys could push her to her full strengths.

Once cross country season was over, the three of us (Colleen, Steve, and I) continued to train. We each had our reasons, but we'll continue Colleen's story first. Since my mother worked at the high school, it was easy for us to run the 5-6 miles to school every morning. I drove over to each of Steve's and Colleen's houses, picked them up, and left the car at my house with our school clothes in the car. Mom drove the car to school while we were running the route. We then got our clothes from the car at school, showered, and were ready for class.

Winter in western Washington State is known as "the Dark Ages." It's cold, damp, rainy. It's dreary and dark. Many were the times when we teenagers didn't feel like running that morning. It was dark and early; we had to run the 5-6 miles and be there in time to shower and be ready for the first class.

The funny thing is, none of us wanted to disappoint the others. We ran to school anyway. We were each accountability partners for the others. We didn't call it that, of course, but that's what we were.

Steve and I, naturally, kept an eye on Colleen's competitions that spring. We knew her body language and running style. We'd been there with her, literally every step of the way that year. She, for her part, had spent her winter running with the varsity.

A typical high school track is a quarter-mile oval. It's two laps for the half-mile, four laps for the mile, and for boys, eight laps for the two-mile run. There are strategies for when to be in front, when to be in the back of the pack, whether to pass on the outside or inside, how to handle moving into or coming out of the turn.

For Colleen, however, there was no strategy. She was so far in front of everyone else that there was nothing to discuss. She wouldn't meet anyone else to challenge her until the state championships. Her only challenge was the stopwatch.

That year, as a junior, she placed fourth in the State of Washington for the half-mile and placed fifth in the mile with a time of 5:42.3. The winning time was 5:35.5. The next year, as a senior, she placed sixth with a time of 5:30.6. If she'd run that time the previous year, she'd have won the event by a clear five seconds!

High school graduation, for Steve and I, was June 7, 1975. That would seem trivial, but it wasn't. Colleen, a junior, was part of the honor guard. She'd be standing on the stage for the whole ceremony while Steve and I sat in the audience, basking in our graduating glory. Or so we thought.

Graduation was in the afternoon. That morning the three of us competed in the Third Annual Sound-to-Narrows 7.5-mile run with plenty of hills. (It's now advertised as Washington State's oldest 12K run.) Colleen, to the best of my recollection, came in first for all prep (high school age) women. After the race, we jumped in the car and zoomed to be ready for graduation. Steve and I both had our leg muscles seize up trying to sit still. We couldn't imagine the agony Colleen was enduring, having to stand still, on stage with everyone watching!

We each had our own reasons for training together that winter. Colleen needed training partners who could keep up with her, even push her. Neither Steve nor I would ever compete in the state finals, but it was fun knowing that she would.

My own reason had nothing to do with track and field. I was preparing for the basketball throw.

I was preparing for the United States Air Force Academy (USAFA)'s arduous admissions process[20] (Figure 2.6). The Physical Aptitude Examination, now called the Candidate Fitness Assessment on the USAFA website, includes a basketball throw. That sounds easy, right? On the contrary, it's weird. It's much like Fizz Buzz.

The basketball throw tests how far you can throw a basketball while kneeling on your knees. It's an unusual motion. You can't use your whole body to achieve distance because your knees must remain straight, behind a line. There's a scooping motion, and a rhythm, needed to throw that basketball for distance. It then takes months to develop the strength behind that motion.

---

[20] *admissions process:* https://www.academyadmissions.com/

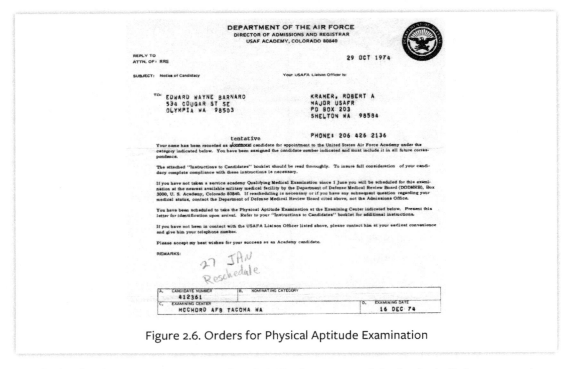

Figure 2.6. Orders for Physical Aptitude Examination

That's why the USAFA can immediately tell who practiced the basketball throw month after month, and who did not. They're seeking the young men and women most determined to pass.

My high school's wrestling coach agreed to set me up with a year-long training program aimed at passing the Physical Aptitude Exam. I wasn't even on the wrestling team! But he was the right person for the individualized program. Always be open to finding the right mentor in unexpected places.

My coach set up the strength training for the pull-ups, push-ups, shuttle run, and sit-ups. We cleared my use of the high school gym for solo rope climbs and tossing all the basketballs from one side of the gym to the other, and back again.

The USAFA is completely clear about their intentions with the assessment. Once you're exhausted from all the strength tests, *then* you'll undertake a one-mile run. *That* is why I was out every morning running to school with Steve and Colleen. Mastering any skill, whether physical or mental, requires planning and practice. Mastery comes when you practice at all times, in all seasons, under all conditions.

Thanks to Steve and Colleen—and the wrestling coach, and mom—come January 27th of my senior year, I passed. Now I had a new goal: Survive Basic Cadet Training which would begin late June. We continued our daily runs to school.

Fizz Buzz Practice

Mastering a skill comes from deliberate, extended, practice. Sometimes the skill is physical, as with Track and Field. Fizz Buzz, though not a physical skill, still takes extended practice. These are the types of coding challenges I've had presented at job interviews 2017-2018; let me share my strategies.

First, come prepared to take a coding challenge. In my case, that means bringing my laptop with me and the reading glasses I use for computer screens. Have a pen or pencil and paper available for writing down Wi-Fi passwords or whatever. I typically use an iPad for notes, but with pencil and paper, I can leave the notes with the interviewer and not break confidentiality concerns. Make sure you have your laptop battery fully charged in case you don't have access to a power outlet.

Rather than jumping straight to writing code, check out the environment and testing structure. Make sure you can run the tests. Make some change (such as an `echo 'hello world';`) and verify the change worked as expected.

In one challenge, the biggest problem was the environment. They had a Cloud9 environment set up so they could watch my typing via a shared screen. The output scrolling didn't work correctly—it disappeared. But I could see something was wrong. I knew it wasn't my code, because I had not written any code yet!

I could have wasted a lot of time figuring out why my code didn't work. Instead, I spent the majority of the "challenge" time figuring out how to make the environment work for me. After that, writing the code was trivial, and we could immediately see it worked.

In two recent coding challenges, the interviewers wanted me to talk through my thought process as I was solving the challenge. I did ask if it would be okay for me to check the online documentation for specific PHP functions; in all cases, the answer was yes. So, relax and talk it through. Assuming all goes well, these people will be your team members. Let them get to know you!

In all cases, it was crucial to have plenty of experience using PHPUnit, the standard unit-testing framework. For example, in some cases, PHPUnit "swallows up" the output. That means `print_r()` and `var_dump()` won't work. What I do is throw an exception and PHPUnit displays the exception message for you:

```
throw new \Exception(print_r($object, true));
```

2. Profile of the "Real Programmer"

Get what information you can beforehand. Ask if there will be a coding challenge, how much time will be needed, will it be pure PHP (or whatever your primary language is), and so on. Ask if they use a specific environment such as HackerRank. Ask if you should be bringing in your laptop.

Are there ways to practice for these sorts of coding challenges? Certainly! Here are some places to start:

- Cloud9[21]—"A cloud IDE for writing, running, and debugging code".
- HackerRank[22]—sign up for a free account and gain experience points for completing challenges.
- LeetCode[23]–they do include Bash scripting and MySQL. They have structured exercises for numerous algorithms.
- Exercism[24]—includes mentorship.
- Project Euler[25]—mathematical/computer programming problems to tackle.

These coding challenges are not aimed at demonstrating your ability to build or scale-out a website. They're giving you the opportunity to demonstrate your use of the target computer programming language.

Free Code Camp analyzed thousands of coding interviews[26] and has several strategies for getting through the coding interview.

The article also notes:

> *Furthermore, no matter what, poor technical ability seems highly correlated with poor communication ability—regardless of language, it's relatively rare for candidates to perform well technically but not effectively communicate what they're doing (or vice versa).*

Skill comes with practice. I gladly recommend finding one or more sites with coding challenges. Get comfortable with the challenges. With practice, you'll develop strategies for how to continue making progress when you get stuck. You can't just think about what you'll do when you get stuck. You need to get stuck, repeatedly, and work through it.

---

[21] *Cloud9: https://aws.amazon.com/cloud9/*
[22] *HackerRank: https://www.hackerrank.com*
[23] *LeetCode: https://leetcode.com*
[24] *Exercism: https://exercism.io*
[25] *Project Euler: https://projecteuler.net*
[26] *analyzed thousands of coding interviews: https://phpa.me/freecodecamp-interviews*

At the same time, practice communicating your thought process as you complete the challenge. Talk out loud to your screen if that's what it takes! Better yet, find an accountability partner. Explain your thought process and what you've learned. The more you communicate, the more you'll internalize what you've learned. Forming a study group or meetup might be a great option, depending on your inclinations.

Your coding challenges are out there. Practice! Get comfortable with that style of writing code. When you're presented a coding challenge during the job interview, show that you can handle it. Skill comes with practice. And, with practice, comes that "been there, done that" confidence that will shine through.

Learning

We've established that we really need to hire people other than Real Programmers. Software developers constantly discuss things like which programming language to use. When arguments begin over which is the *best* programming language, the standard PHP joke runs like this:

> *Question: What do you call a good PHP developer?*
>
> *Answer: Employed.*

The answer's the same for Real Programmers, though for different reasons. Real Programmers, because of their weird relationship to the computers themselves, will always find employment. When you find a Real Programmer who does PHP, now *that* will be weird.

Can we learn from a Real Programmer without being a Real Programmer? Certainly! You might not be practiced, for example, in converting decimal numbers to hexadecimal, in your head, without computers or calculators. We'll fix that. It's fun!

Do you need that skill? You already know the answer—no. But what you should know is the underlying skill. We'll be learning how to design an algorithm in our heads. In the world of computers and software, that is a useful skill. We'll learn the skill by playing hexadecimal in our heads.

The rest of this book, then, shares the journey. We'll meet some Real Programmers along the way. We'll be picking up some of their skills. We'll be learning the "skill behind the skill," so to speak. It's those skills, I have found, that last a lifetime.

Summary

Much of our industry's selection process is based on the *Fizz Buzz* premise that most people "can't program their way out of a wet paper bag." Our industry's ongoing existence proves this to be a mistaken premise.

We are selecting for what I call the "Real Programmer" profile. Our industry needs to do far more than merely "stacking the deck" with Real Programmers. Be that as it may, the "Real Programmer" types do have an intimate understanding of how computers and software work. Since I fit that profile, at least to some extent, we'll be learning what skills *I* can share along those lines.

Chapter

3

Think Like a Computer

There's a skill fundamental to software development I've always found useful. This skill is essential when working with *every* programming language, including PHP and when working across PHP frameworks. Like all skills, mastery comes from study and practice.

What is this skill? It's learning to think like a computer and to view software from the computer's perspective. We'll first see how I learned the skill way back when—that's part of the story—and then learn about a Kickstarter product which teaches this very skill. We'll even discuss how beginners can practice this skill with just HTML and CSS.

3. Think Like a Computer

I have been trying, for two years now, to explain and teach a particular software development skill. I've missed it every time. It's more subtle, more fundamental than I recognized.

We'll need to travel back to when I began to learn this mysterious skill. I'll show you what this skill appears to be. I'll show you how to acquire this skill. Is the skill important today? I believe so, and I'll explain that too.

Dr. Heather D. Pfeiffer, in her 2001 lecture notes for CS 273[1] (Machine Programming and Organization), writes:

> *Computers work through a serendipitous interplay of four developments:*
>
> - *Binary arithmetic*
> - *Boolean logic (developed by George Boole)*
> - *Digital electronics (originally based on relays for telephone company applications)*
> - *Computability theory (especially Turing and Goedel)*
>
> *We are interested in the first three items.*

I learned radix arithmetic[2] in primary school. I was around nine years old, in 4th or 5th grade. We learned to convert from standard base-10 numbers to base-12, base-2, or whatever number system we needed to. We learned simple addition and subtraction in the alternate number system. That skill is no longer (as far as I know) taught in primary school. Is it an important skill? Perhaps not; it's not a skill used day-to-day.

It is, however, a skill I have used throughout my career, so I have assumed it's crucial. Yet, software gets developed without actual working knowledge of binary or hexadecimal arithmetic. So, it's not *the* important skill, even though it's a useful skill.

I was nine when I took a pair of summer enrichment classes; one was cryptography. I was excited about that one! However, to my surprise, most of that session involved matrix multiplication[3]. I had a rough time with matrix multiplication and could not make the connection from matrix multiplication to cryptography. I still don't know the connection! What did I learn? I learned I would never become a professional cryptographer, not with all that math.

---

[1] CS 273: https://phpa.me/nmsu-binary
[2] radix arithmetic: https://en.wikipedia.org/wiki/Radix
[3] matrix multiplication: https://phpa.me/matrix-multiplication

The other summer school class was about Boolean logic or Boolean algebra. That sounded like math, so I didn't know if I'd like it or not. But, it related to computers in some way so I hoped it would be fun. It was.

It was easy enough to understand AND, OR, and NOT "gates" (operators), and from those gates construct NAND and NOR. Two inputs and one output defined each gate. Everything was consistent. It was like knowing three plus two always produces five. Add three and two, or two and three, and the result is always five. Every time. To me, this made sense.

But then we did something I'd never seen before. We connected these logic gates in a sequence, one after another. We learned equivalent expressions, such as (a or b) inverted produces (not-a and not-b), while (a and b) inverted produces (not-a or not-b). When inverting, swap the "and" for "or" and vice versa using de Morgan's Theorem[4]. We drew out the diagrams to prove this.

We also had a rudimentary plugboard where we could physically wire up the logic gates, one gate propagating (cascading) to the next. There was a little light bulb showing the state of each input and each output. We could see the whole thing.

The whole thing was totally awesome. I could *see* what was happening. Therefore each piece or step made sense. I did not really understand why negating a Boolean term means swapping "and" for "or," but I could see that it did. If someone could articulate the rules, I could follow the rules. For example, I already knew the commutative property[5] of addition states that three plus two produces the same result as two plus three. We can swap the operands with each other without altering the result.

In other words, "a plus b" equals "b plus a." I could immediately transfer that knowledge to Boolean algebra: "a AND b" equals "b AND a," and "a OR b" equals "b OR a." The material was presented in such a way that I could bridge the gap from arithmetic to Boolean logic.

Then came the gap I couldn't bridge.

---

[4] de Morgan's Theorem: https://phpa.me/wikip-de-morgans
[5] commutative property: https://phpa.me/wikip-commutative

Popular Electronics

Popular Electronics magazine (April 1968)[6] published *Demonstrating Binary Computation with the Binary Adder* (Figure 3.1). It was a 4-bit binary adder! I was able to draw out the logic diagram[7] on paper, but this was the actual electrical circuit built with resistors, diodes, switches, and lights. Mom drove me around to electrical supply stores to get the necessary discrete parts, and Dad helped me with the soldering. I became fascinated with the colored bands on resistors because they encrypted coefficient, mantissa, degree of precision, and range of error.

I built the thing. Figure 3.2 shows me demonstrating the 4-bit binary adder with my sister Vicki on the left.

I was quite proud of the thing. Nobody else in my grade school had built their computer from loose parts. I could explain *what* it did, and *why*, but I could not explain *how* it worked. I had learned how to draw out the logic diagram for a binary adder the previous summer, and I knew this computer was a physical implementation of that diagram (Figure 3.3). But there was nothing I could point to inside the thing and say, "That's the AND gate." I could point to the wire representing the carry bit ("CARRY IN" at the upper right of Figure 3.3), and I could point to the wires representing the input (the switches on the front). But I could not explain how the electrical circuit got from input to output. I could follow the circuit from the ground symbol at the bottom of Figure 3.3 to the neon output light at the top (marked NE2H). But I could not match that electronic circuit diagram to the equivalent Boolean logic diagram (Figure 3.4). There was a gap in knowledge, and I never did bridge that gap.

Have we found that elusive skill? We're getting close. Remember, Dr. Pfeiffer said computers work because of binary arithmetic, Boolean logic, and digital electronics. We just demonstrated all three. But should we be searching out some obscure project from 1968? Certainly not. We can do better. And, by the way, the elusive skill is not any of these three. It's not binary arithmetic, Boolean logic, or digital circuitry.

Let's close out the flashback and return to today.

---

[6]   *Popular Electronics magazine (April 1968):* https://phpa.me/poptronics-1968-pdf
[7]   *logic diagram:* https://phpa.me/wikip-full-adder

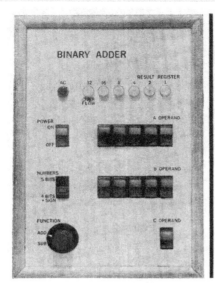

Figure 3.1. Binary Adder project

Figure 3.2. Four-bit binary adder

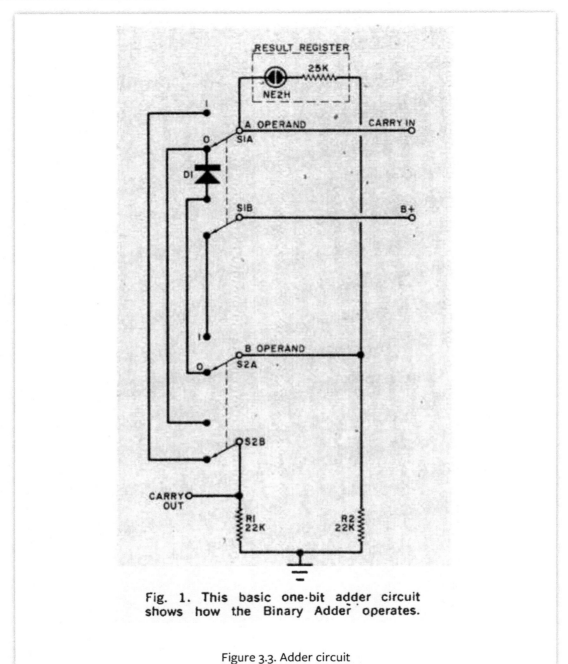

Fig. 1. This basic one·bit adder circuit shows how the Binary Adder operates.

Figure 3.3. Adder circuit

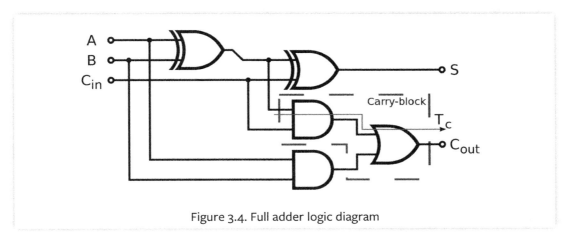

Figure 3.4. Full adder logic diagram

Turing Tumble

Almost precisely 50 years later, Paul Boswell created a Kickstarter campaign called Turing Tumble[8]. The $48,000 goal received more than $400,000 pledged. (I have no relationship to the product or its creators.) We'll be using Turing Tumble, but not for its stated purpose.

Boswell explains,

> *I'm all about teaching kids to code. When I was a professor at the University of Minnesota, I saw how valuable it is for all students to be coders. I have three young kids and I've tried all sorts of games to build their interest in coding. The problem is that they all treat computers like abstract, black boxes. They overlook the fundamental, incredible concept: how simple switches, connected together in clever ways, can do incredibly smart things.*
>
> *Kids learn best when they use their senses to explore concepts. Turing Tumble is the only game that lets kids see and feel how computers work. The logic isn't hidden inside a computer chip—it's all right there in front of them. It builds logic and critical thinking skills, fundamental coding concepts, and grounds their understanding of computers.*
>
> *And adults, this game is not just for kids!*
>
> *It's a game unlike any you've ever played. It takes creative thinking to come up with a solution to each puzzle—you can't just stumble across the solution by trial and error—and it's extremely gratifying to build it and watch it work. Even if you're an expert programmer, I guarantee you'll find the latter puzzles a challenge.*

---

[8]   Turing Tumble: https://www.turingtumble.com

I missed the Kickstarter, but went down to Games by James and purchased a copy for $70 (Figure 3.5). It's as good as advertised if you look past its simplicity. The game is packaged as a graphic novel with a storyline, laying out the quest with 60 puzzles to solve. The game implements such fundamental concepts as AND, OR, bits, registers, addition, counting, and loops. The game is Turing Complete[9], meaning that with a big enough playing board, and enough parts, we could implement any digital algorithm.

Figure 3.6 shows Challenge 56, which is to design a multiplication circuit. The lower-left frame illustrates the starting setup. Use any parts needed from the list at the lower right to design the circuit flow.

Let's first look at the situation for an eight to 10-year-old, then as professional software developers. There's an important skill hidden here, but we need a bit more analysis to get there.

Figure 3.5. Running Turing Tumble puzzle 8

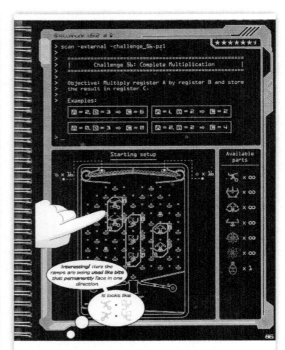

Figure 3.6. Multiplication Circuit (licensed Creative Commons 4.0)

---

[9] Turing Complete: https://phpa.me/wikip-turing-complete

Crypto

Do you recall my describing the cryptography class I took when I was nine? I had such hopes—and the matrix multiplication dashed them. I couldn't do it. But a few years later, in college physics, those struggles helped me to understand dot products. When I realized, in computer science, the implementation can be a multi-dimensional array, I was home free. Countless memory-related or data-related concepts tied back to my attempts to learn cryptography in grade school.

For an eight to 10-year-old, Turing Tumble is a similar situation. I could learn to create patterns resulting in AND, OR, loops, and counting, but I wouldn't be able to make the leap from the plastic pieces and gravity power to how the silicon chip works sitting unseen in the IBM cloud. Or, looking in the other direction as a child, I couldn't make the leap from the binary fundamentals to designing an interactive webpage. There's a gap.

Or is there? Let's look at another example.

When adults want to "learn coding" and wonder where to start, I suggest they begin by learning to hand-code webpages. I explain that HTML and CSS are, in fact, programming languages. They are providing instructions for your browser to execute. Webpages (when just HTML and CSS) are plain text and thus easy to see, create, edit. But the most critical point is, for anyone who asks, they are already familiar with how webpages work.

Webpages, in that sense, provide a comfort level. We've all dealt with webpages at their best and their worst, with good internet connections and bad. We understand what they do and how they work. Thus, as we are learning to create one by hand-coding the markup and styles, we can "bridge the gap" and understand the result.

In the same way, the more we gain experience with what computers do, the better we can bridge the gap between the extreme fundamentals (taught by Turing Tumble) and actual computer hardware.

Here's *my* takeaway. By learning these fundamentals at age eight to 10, it becomes possible to "bridge" all sorts of gaps throughout one's career. The intuitive leaps happen because of prior knowledge. How do I know this is the case? Because of those summer classes and building that binary adder. That's why I told the story, so you'd know why I'm certain Turing Tumble is useful training for your career.

According to Dr. Pfeiffer, computers work through a serendipitous interplay of four developments: binary arithmetic, Boolean logic, digital electronics, and computability theory. Turing Tumble teaches those first three areas through its series of 60 ever-more-challenging, hands-on puzzles. That's great, but do those three areas represent the skills we need in our day-to-day software development? No.

There's something else. It's so simple you might get angry that I took so long to explain it.

Flow

As software developers, we can understand (in theory) any particular piece of code. It might calculate the square root of a number, for example. We know what that means. We know its constraints (input must be non-negative and less than the maximum available floating-point number; output is limited to a certain number of digits' precision). We can look at the code listing and see how it implements the algorithm.

Note that I'm describing the code as a *thing* not a *journey*. We think of the code as producing a result. On the other hand, a great way to understand the code would be to run through the calculation using a pencil and paper. Walk through the algorithm step by step, doing each calculation to the last digit, and no further, at every step. Mark Twain explained there is no substitute for first-hand experience:

> *If you hold a cat by the tail, you learn things that cannot be learned in any other way.*

None of us is in the habit of walking through every piece of software, doing every step by hand. Even with tools like XDebug available, we don't step through our code every time! That's why we have computers. (By the same thinking, none of us needs to test our software; that's why we have users.) Instead, we *look* at the software and recognize what it *does*. There's a gap here. It's subtle. But Turing Tumble can help bridge that gap.

Computers run on electricity, that is, electrons flowing through circuits. The Turing Tumble computer runs on falling marbles running through circuits. We can't see the electrons, but we can watch the marbles. Where electricity takes only two nanoseconds to travel through a foot of circuitry, the marble takes several seconds to travel that same distance through the Turing Tumble circuitry.

Because the electronic computer is so nearly instantaneous (unless using JavaScript), I can only picture the computer's *result*. I don't visualize the *flow* that got us there. I focus on the result rather than the journey. However, the bugs tend to hide in the journey rather than the result.

Each of the 60 Turing Tumble puzzles asks you to design a flow which achieves a result. Once designed, you then press "start" and watch the flow. The flow is the solution. The result merely confirms that you achieved the correct flow.

Turing Tumble teaches that computers work because electrons flow. That's great to know, but how does that help with modern software development? We're almost to that subtle skill; in fact, we've arrived.

Journey Versus Destination

What's the big secret? It's thinking about software in terms of flow rather than the result. I don't mean the flow of *data* through a system; I mean the flow of the *processor* (CPU and friends) executing your instructions (the software).

Is binary arithmetic essential to day-to-day software development? Not usually. But learning how computers do binary arithmetic leads to understanding how computers process instructions.

We understand how flow-of-control works through a piece of software. We can read an if/else test. We know a loop runs a certain number of times, and then flow continues past the loop. We know that, given "these" input conditions, a square-root function produces "that" output result.

But all of that is at a relatively high level. The subtle skill here is the more intimate understanding. Think of the flow at a more fundamental level.

Software development is, in essence, instructing computers how to do things. Thus, it's important to understand how computers carry out those instructions. If you instruct the computer to add "one-third plus one-third plus one-third," the answer probably won't be the number one. It will be a number very slightly less than one because that's how computers work.

Software development is also, in essence, designing a flow to achieve a result. When we write software, we're describing the flow. When the computer runs the software, what does it do? It flows. Electrons flow. The CPU (and friends such as GPU, instruction bus, etc.) flows. Program control flows. When the computer is running software, it's literally the journey, not the destination.

What's the secret skill? It's to think as a computer does. Form empathy, so to speak. Look at your software from a computer's point of view, not a person's point of view.

If you were to write a cookbook for children, for example, you would need to visualize how a child would follow your recipe and cooking instructions. You need to get past how *you*, as an adult, would implement the recipe, and instead follow the instructions as if you were the target audience. That can be difficult, depending on your level of empathy.

3. THINK LIKE A COMPUTER

It can be equally challenging to look at your software—or anyone's software—from a computer's perspective, to think in terms of the computer's processing flow. It takes a certain level of empathy. Each Turing Tumble puzzle, in that sense, is an empathy-first design.

Skill comes with practice. The skill here is to visualize the processing flow from the computer's perspective. Have fun! Fun is important, and keeps the boredom at bay:

> *"Look. My job's pretty simple," Randy says. "There's that big cable from Taiwan down to Luzon. A router at each end. Then there's the network of short-run, inter-island cables that the other people are laying in the Philippines. Each cable segment begins and ends at a router, as you know. My job is to program the routers, make sure that the data will have a clear path from Taiwan to here."*
>
> *John Cantrell glances away, worried that he's about to get bored. Randy practically lunges across the table, because he knows it's not boring. "John! you are a major credit card company!"*
>
> *"Okay." Cantrell meets his gaze, slightly unnerved.*
>
> *"You are storing your data in the data haven we're building. You need to download a terabyte of crucial data. You begin the process—your encrypted bytes are screaming up through the Philippines at a gigabyte per second, to Taiwan, from there across to the States." Randy pauses and swigs Guinness, building the drama. "Then, a ferry capsizes off Cebu."*
>
> *"So?"*
>
> *"So, in the space of ten minutes, a hundred thousand Filipinos all pick up their telephones simultaneously."*
>
> *Cantrell actually whacks his forehead. "Oh, my god!"*
>
> *"Now you understand! I've been configuring this network so that no matter what happens, the data continues to flow to that credit-card company. Maybe at a reduced speed—but it flows."*
>
> *—Cryptonomicon (1999) by Neal Stephenson (p. 307)*

We all visualize sequences of events. We can picture the result of that (fictional) ferry capsizing off Cebu. It caused an overwhelming traffic spike. Get in the habit of visualizing the events with all software, and you'll develop a valuable skill for all software development.

Summary

It's a tricky undertaking to think of software the way the computer thinks about the software. The key is to think about the flow rather than the result. Picture the journey rather than the destination. Seeing the destination is easy; it's right in front of you. Seeing the journey is the subtle skill to be developed. I'm particularly pleased with Turing Tumble because it provides a way to see, picture, study, and internalize the journey. With practice, the perspective becomes second nature.

Chapter

4

The Basics With a Side of Crypto

In this chapter we'll be learning to think like the computer does. Toward this end, we'll learn to use Boolean logic, ones' complement notation, and two's complement notation. We'll be walking through some modern (2019) PHP code. This chapter would be nearly identical programming C, and likely the same in any other C-like language.

If I were to render my own 50+ years of studying and programming computers down to a single chapter, it would be this chapter. We'll be taking a couple of lines of code—just two lines—and working through the calculation as a computer does. Is the actual calculation important? No. Is the binary arithmetic, in itself, important? No. What's important is coming to understand how a computer thinks, that is, understanding how the computer processes code that we write. What's our path to that understanding? You guessed it; we'll be using binary arithmetic and Boolean logic.

Crypto Problem

Our mission is to transform information in a way that's resistant to known attacks. Our particular concern is called the *cache-timing attack*[1]. If different strings, all the same length, take different times to transform, this potentially leaks information about the string's contents. With precise measurements of the time for each operation, an attacker can work backward to the input. This technique is known as a timing attack[2].

By "transform" I mean convert arbitrary information (raw binary data) to an ASCII string. It's the same idea as base-64 encoding[3]. We'll call this transformation "encoding" for the rest of the chapter.

The solution is to engage in constant-time encoding (that is, constant for a given input-data length) regardless of the input-data content.

This chapter is not about cryptography. It's about binary arithmetic and Boolean logic. I pulled an example from active modern-day cryptography to provide us a realistic context.

What We'll Learn

We'll be using PHP, however, the calculations will be identical for the C language and likely similar for any other C-like language. We'll be doing mathematical (binary) operations, and the syntax will be the same. The rest of this chapter uses PHP syntax and terminology.

What we'll learn:

- The PHP bitwise operators & ("bitwise and"), | ("bitwise or"), ~ ("bitwise not"), ^ ("bitwise exclusive or"), << ("shift left"), >> ("shift right") work with ones' complement representation[4].

- PHP integer arithmetic works with two's complement representation[5].

[1] cache-timing attack: *https://blog.ircmaxell.com/2014/11/its-all-about-time.html*
[2] timing attack: *https://en.wikipedia.org/wiki/Timing_attack*
[3] base-64 encoding: *https://en.wikipedia.org/wiki/Base64*
[4] ones' complement representation: *http://phpa.me/wikip-ones-complement*
[5] two's complement representation: *https://phpa.me/wikip-twos-complement*

- It's perfectly valid, but weird, to combine the two in the same calculation.

- Once we can tell the difference between integer arithmetic and logical operations, it becomes easy.

The PHP language does include the keywords AND, OR, and XOR. These keywords are *logical* operators and have nothing to do with the above-listed *bitwise* operators. Do not confuse the AND operator with the *bitwise AND* operator &. We'll *only* be using the bitwise operators in this chapter. See the PHP language documentation of operators[6] for exact detail.

The Library

We'll examine a few lines of code from the Constant Time Encoding[7] library.

Listing 4.1 is extracted from Hex.php[8]. We'll encode a binary string into hexadecimal-digit characters. To keep this simple, we'll encode a one-letter string.

Listing 4.1. Hex

```
1.  <?php
2.  declare(strict_types=1);
3.
4.  namespace ParagonIE\ConstantTime;
5.
6.  /**
7.   * Copyright (c) 2016 - 2018 Paragon Initiative Enterprises.
8.   * Copyright (c) 2014 Steve "Sc00bz" Thomas (steve at tobtu dot com)
9.   *
10.  * Permission is hereby granted, free of charge, to any person obtaining a copy
11.  * of this software and associated documentation files (the "Software"), to deal
12.  * in the Software without restriction, including without limitation the rights
13.  * to use, copy, modify, merge, publish, distribute, sublicense, and/or sell
14.  * copies of the Software, and to permit persons to whom the Software is
15.  * furnished to do so, subject to the following conditions:
16.  *
17.  * The above copyright notice and this permission notice shall be included in all
18.  * copies or substantial portions of the Software.
19.  *
20.  * THE SOFTWARE IS PROVIDED "AS IS", WITHOUT WARRANTY OF ANY KIND, EXPRESS OR
21.  * IMPLIED, INCLUDING BUT NOT LIMITED TO THE WARRANTIES OF MERCHANTABILITY,
22.  * FITNESS FOR A PARTICULAR PURPOSE AND NONINFRINGEMENT. IN NO EVENT SHALL THE
23.  * AUTHORS OR COPYRIGHT HOLDERS BE LIABLE FOR ANY CLAIM, DAMAGES OR OTHER
24.  * LIABILITY, WHETHER IN AN ACTION OF CONTRACT, TORT OR OTHERWISE, ARISING FROM,
25.  * OUT OF OR IN CONNECTION WITH THE SOFTWARE OR THE USE OR OTHER DEALINGS IN THE
```

---

[6] operators: *https://php.net/language.operators*
[7] Constant Time Encoding: *https://phpa.me/paragonie-cte*
[8] Hex.php: *https://phpa.me/paragonie-cte-hex*

```
26.   *   SOFTWARE.
27.   */
28.
29.  /**
30.   * Class Hex
31.   *
32.   * @package ParagonIE\ConstantTime
33.   */
34.  abstract class Hex implements EncoderInterface {
35.      /**
36.       * Convert a binary string into a hexadecimal string without cache-timing
37.       * leaks
38.       *
39.       * @param string $binString (raw binary)
40.       * @return string
41.       * @throws \TypeError
42.       */
43.      public static function encode(string $binString): string {
44.          /** @var string $hex */
45.          $hex = '';
46.          $len = Binary::safeStrlen($binString);
47.          for ($i = 0; $i < $len; ++$i) {
48.              /** @var array<int, int> $chunk */
49.              $chunk = \unpack('C', Binary::safeSubstr($binString, $i, 1));
50.              /** @var int $c */
51.              $c = $chunk[1] & 0xf;
52.              /** @var int $b */
53.              $b = $chunk[1] >> 4;
54.
55.              $hex .= pack(
56.                  'CC',
57.                  (87 + $b + ((($b - 10) >> 8) & ~38)),
58.                  (87 + $c + ((($c - 10) >> 8) & ~38))
59.              );
60.          }
61.          return $hex;
62.      }
63.  }
```

Numbering Systems

Do we commonly use numbering systems such as hexadecimal? Yes, we do! Web CSS (Cascading Style Sheet) specifies colors as numbers. CSS color specifications are either six hexadecimal digits or three decimal numbers. The decimal number ranging from 0 to 255 (0..255) corresponds to the hexadecimal number 0..ff. CSS allows a shorthand where #ffffff becomes #fff.

Figure 4.1. Sample Colors

Figure 4.1. Sample Colors

Figure 4.1 shows representative colors with their hexadecimal and decimal (RGB, meaning Red-Green-Blue) representation. We won't discuss CSS any further; the point here is that you may have already encountered hexadecimal numbers by working with CSS colors.

We'll be looking at the ASCII character set. It too is represented as decimal numbers (0..255) and hexadecimal numbers (0x0..0xff), but also in binary.

To get started, let's look at the first seven ASCII characters. They're "control characters" dating from the teletype days. Their meaning doesn't matter to us; we only care that they're represented by the decimal numbers zero through six (0..6).

Figure 4.2 shows how we count the same numbers in binary notation: 0 (zero), 1 (one), 10 (two), 11 (three), 100 (four), 101 (five), 110 (six).

Decimal	Octal	Hex	Binary	Value	Description
000	000	000	0000 0000	NUL	"null" character
001	001	001	0000 0001	SOH	start of header
002	002	002	0000 0010	STX	start of text
003	003	003	0000 0011	ETX	end of text
004	004	004	0000 0100	EOT	end of transmission
005	005	005	0000 0101	ENQ	enquiry
006	006	006	0000 0110	ACK	acknowledgement

Figure 4.2. ASCII 000-006

Figure 4.3 shows how we count in octal. We count from zero to seven, then skip to 010. (PHP notation uses a leading zero for octal notation, a leading 0x for hexadecimal notation, and a leading 0b for binary notation.)

Decimal	Octal	Hex	Binary	Value	Description
007	007	007	0000 0111	BEL	bell
008	010	008	0000 1000	BS	backspace
009	011	009	0000 1001	TAB	horizontal tab
010	012	00a	0000 1010	LF	line feed
011	013	00b	0000 1011	VT	vertical tab
012	014	00c	0000 1100	FF	form feed
013	015	00d	0000 1101	CR	carriage return
014	016	00e	0000 1110	SO	shift in
015	017	00f	0000 1111	SI	shift out

Figure 4.3. ASCII 007-015

The hexadecimal numbers run from zero through nine, then continue 0xa through 0xf. 0x10 comes after 0xf.

Note the ASCII letter "Q" (Figure 4.4). It's represented in decimal as 81, octal 0121, hexadecimal 0x51, and binary 0101 0001 (space added for clarity).

Decimal	Octal	Hex	Binary	Value
079	117	04f	0100 1111	O
080	120	050	0101 0000	P
081	121	051	0101 0001	Q
082	122	052	0101 0010	R
083	123	053	0101 0011	S
084	124	054	0101 0100	T

Figure 4.4. ASCII Q

We're going to encode the string "Q" using Hex::encode(). Refer back to the for loop in our listing. Since our string length is one (the string is a single character), we're taking one and only one trip through the loop.

We can, therefore, focus on the code inside the for loop. It's effectively straight-line code, that is, it doesn't loop. There are only four statements inside the loop, so this will be easy, right? Not exactly! That's why we're here.

First, we unpack:

```
/** @var array<int, int> $chunk */
$chunk = \unpack('C', Binary::safeSubstr($binString, $i, 1));
```

The first question we should ask is, how do unpack() and Binary::safeSubstr() work? A quick check of Binary.php[9] in the Constant Time Encoding library shows it is a wrapper for PHP's "choose a substring" functions. It works as we would expect (Listing 4.2).

Listing 4.2. Safe Substring

```
1.  <?php
2.  abstract class Binary {
3.      public static function safeSubstr(
4.          string $str,
5.          int $start = 0,
6.          $length = null
7.      ): string {
8.          if ($length === 0) {
9.              return '';
10.         }
11.         if (\function_exists('mb_substr')) {
12.             return \mb_substr($str, $start, $length, '8bit');
13.         }
14.         // Unlike mb_substr(), substr() doesn't accept NULL for length
15.         if ($length !== null) {
16.             return \substr($str, $start, $length);
17.         } else {
18.             return \substr($str, $start);
19.         }
20.     }
21. }
```

The official unpack[10] documentation tells us the 'C' formatting is for unsigned (8-bit) characters. That's what we want.

---

[9] Binary.php: https://phpa.me/paragonie-cte-binary
[10] unpack: http://php.net/function.unpack

However, it pays to be careful. If we scroll far enough down the online documentation page, we'll see this warning:

> **Caution** *If you do not name an element, numeric indices starting from 1 are used. Be aware that if you have more than one unnamed element, some data is overwritten because the numbering restarts from 1 for each element.*

Yes, we can use unpack in such a way that it overwrites its own output. Remember this feature as we examine our next line of code.

```
/** @var int $c */
$c = $chunk[1] & 0xf;
```

We unpacked our string into array $chunk. Zero is normally the first index in a PHP array. But, as cautioned above, unpack sets the array index to start from one. The PHP libraries are consistently inconsistent about things like this; keep a close eye on the documentation!

Before we go any further, however, we need to learn more about the bitwise operations. We're using PHP syntax, but the concepts are the same for any of the C family of programming languages.

Logical Operations

Here is the bitwise AND truth table (in PHP, this is the & operator, not to be confused with PHP's AND operator). A truth table is a way of expressing "these inputs produce these outputs, always, in all cases."

```
1  1  0  0    Left operand
1  0  1  0    Right operand
----------    & (bitwise AND)
1  0  0  0    Result
```

In this case, we've arranged the truth table vertically. Read each column to get a true statement for bitwise AND:

- $1 \& 1 = 1$
- $1 \& 0 = 0$
- $0 \& 1 = 0$
- $0 \& 0 = 0$

If the left and right operand are both true, the result is true. In all other cases, the result is false. In truth tables, true is usually shown as 1 and false as 0.

Computer hardware normally works with multi-bit numbers. The calculation might look like this:

```
// 0b1000 === (0b1100 & 0b1010)
$result = $left & $right;
```

Now we can complete our two lines of code:

```
/** @var array<int, int> $chunk */
$chunk = \unpack('C', Binary::safeSubstr($binString, $i, 1));
/** @var int $c */
$c = $chunk[1] & 0xf;
```

Our string contained the letter "Q", which is represented by decimal 81 or hexadecimal 0x51. We, therefore, know that $chunk[1] contains 0x51.

Let's do the bitwise AND calculation for $c = $chunk[1] & 0xf;:

```
0101 0001    $chunk[1] === 0x51 === 'Q'
0000 1111    0xf
---------
0000 0001    $c = $chunk[1] & 0xf;
```

Our binary calculation with the bitwise AND operator tells us:

```
$chunk = 0x51; // Ascii Q
$c = 1;        // Rightmost hex digit
```

Let's take on our third line of code:

```
/** @var array<int, int> $chunk */
$chunk = \unpack('C', Binary::safeSubstr($binString, $i, 1));
/** @var int $c */
$c = $chunk[1] & 0xf;
/** @var int $b */
$b = $chunk[1] >> 4;
```

The expression >> 4 means to take the left operand, which is $chunk[1], and shift the left operand four positions (in binary) to the right. The PHP documentation for bitwise operators[11] tells us "right shifts have copies of the sign bit shifted in on the left, meaning the sign of an operand is preserved."

---

[11] bitwise operators: http://php.net/language.operators.bitwise

We look at what that means later in this chapter. For now, just be aware that when shifting to the right, the leftmost bit is propagated to the right. If the leftmost bit is 0, we'll have four zeroes brought in from the left as part of the right shift. If the leftmost bit is 1, we'll have four ones brought in from the left.

```
0101 0001    $chunk[1] === 0x51
    >> 4     Shift 4 bits to the right
---------
0000 0101    $b = $chunk[1] >> 4;
```

We now have:

```
$chunk = 0x51; // Ascii Q
$c = 1;        // Right hex digit
$b = 5;        // Left hex digit
```

The operations we just performed are called *shifting and masking*. The *mask* 0xf (binary 0000 1111), by virtue of having the rightmost four bits set, allowed us to extract a four-bit value, namely the rightmost hexadecimal digit. Given that we began with an 8-bit value (the result of unpacking with the 'C' format) we can obtain the other four-bit value by shifting to the right.

Now it's time to learn ones' complement and two's complement arithmetic.

Figure 4.5

Ones' Complement Arithmetic

Seymour Cray's CDC 6600 (Figure 4.5)—the first successful supercomputer—used ones' complement arithmetic. This was in 1964. Its circuits were cooled by extensive chilled water plumbing.

The following listing is a chart showing ones' complement representation, in binary, for 8-bit words. The principle would be the same for 16-bit, 24-bit, 36-bit, 40-bit, or 60-bit word sizes. (The PDP-10 had a 36-bit word size and Cray's CDC 6600 used a 60-bit word size.) Of course, the larger word size means a correspondingly larger numeric range for integers.

```
 1.       Bits  Logical Value    Arithmetic Value
 2.    (8-bit)     (unsigned)   (ones' complement)
 3. 0111 1111            127                   127
 4. 0111 1110            126                   126
 5. 0000 0010              2                     2 <-- see below
 6. 0000 0001              1             1
 7. 0000 0000              0                     0 <-- "plus zero"
 8. 1111 1111            255                    -0 <-- "minus zero"
 9. 1111 1110            254                    -1
10. 1111 1101            253                    -2 <-- see below
11. 1000 0001            129                  -126
12. 1000 0000            128                  -127
13.
14. For example, 2 and -2 show the bits flipped on each other:
15. 0000 0010              2                     2
16. 1111 1101            253                    -2
```

Modern computers generally do not use ones' complement arithmetic. So why are we learning this? Because the Boolean (bitwise) operators, shifting and masking and so on, use the one's complement representation.

To the computer, a number is just a number. It's a bit pattern somewhere in the hardware. It doesn't care whether we consider that bit pattern to be part of a string, a floating-point number, unsigned integer, or whatever.

The computer begins to care when we begin to *transform* or *operate* on that bit pattern. If we're asking the computer to do a floating-point calculation, the computer will treat that bit pattern as a floating-point number. When we're instructing the computer to perform shifting and masking, it's best to think of that bit pattern as a ones' complement integer.

How big is the ones' complement integer? That depends on the computer's word size. On the CDC 6600, it was 60 bits wide. On modern 64-bit machines, it will be 64 bits wide.

Ones' complement representation works like this:

- 0 is all zeroes in binary

- -0 is all ones in binary

- The "invert operator" (in PHP, the ~ operator) says to flip all the bits, that is, change every 0 to a 1 and change every 1 to a 0

- "All the bits" depends on the computer's word size (32-bit, 64-bit, etc.)

Two's Complement Arithmetic

The IBM System/360 brought two's complement arithmetic to the masses in 1964, the same year as the CDC 6600 and its ones' complement arithmetic. Figure 4.6 shows an IBM System 360/20 computer on display at the Deutsches Museum in Munich Germany. The front panels are removed. An IBM 2560 MFCM (multi-function Card Machine) is shown on the right and the corner of a 2203 printer is visible on the left.

Before we take on two's complement arithmetic, let's get a perspective on the state of business computing. In the mid-1960s, mainframe computers were a big deal. They represented a massive investment by the companies, universities, and government agencies who purchased them. They took up entire rooms—and those rooms were considered showpieces.

Figure 4.6

The computer rooms were spotless and orderly. Every computer room, with those signature white raised-floor tiles, looked just like the sales brochure. The company CEO could—and did—show up at any moment, personally conducting a tour of the computer room for visiting dignitaries.

The Safeco Insurance Company was founded in Seattle, Washington. By the 1960s its office, the Safeco Building was in the University District, where a decade later I was learning to program the CDC 6400.

Across the bridge was Sam's Tavern where the owner, Sam, sang in a barbershop quartet. He often sang the then-popular song "When the Red, Red Robin Comes Bob, Bob, Bobbin Along" and eventually changed the tavern name to Sam's Red Robin. That tavern was purchased, the name Sam dropped, and became the first Red Robin restaurant. I worked out more than one computer programming assignment over a burger at the original Red Robin restaurant!

Let's get back to Safeco. My father Gene Barnard was an internal auditor for Safeco from 1960 onwards. He became the Chief Auditor a year later, 1961, "managing the company's internal audit program and staff, recruiting and training personnel, planning new programs, advising management on internal controls and operational weaknesses." This is perfectly normal "management-speak." Then, it gets weird.

Two years later, in early 1963 as Chief Auditor, Gene made recommendations concerning Safeco's data processing operations. Remember that room-sized computers in the early 1960s were a big deal. IBM was just beginning to embrace the concept and sales pressure was strong.

Safeco was so impressed with Gene's recommendations that they placed him—an auditor by training—in charge of all data processing operations, including the home office and ten regional data processing operations. That's weird. He remained a data processing manager (what we would now call CTO, Chief Technical Officer) for the rest of his lifetime.

What's weirder—to me—is that Dad never mentioned to me that he had been trained in programming the IBM 305, 1401, 7070, and System/360 computers. The IBM RAMAC 305[12] used vacuum tubes. Wikipedia reports, "Programming the 305 involved not only writing machine language instructions to be stored on the drum memory, but also almost every unit in the system (including the computer itself) could be programmed by inserting wire jumpers into a plugboard control panel."

---

[12] IBM RAMAC 305: https://en.wikipedia.org/wiki/IBM_305_RAMAC

RAMAC stood for "Random Access Method of Accounting and Control". This was a plugboard and machine-language computer designed for assisting real-time accounting in business.

One more boring fact leads us to our anecdote. It's hard to think of IBM as a fledgling computer company, and Seattle-based Safeco insurance company as a big deal, but that's how it was in 1965. Dad represented Safeco to IBM in New York "developing a package of computer programs for the fire and casualty insurance industry known as PALIS." JoAnne Yates reports[13] "While the 360 quickly became overwhelmingly successful, the insurance software systems written for it by IBM in 1965—ALIS (Advanced Life Insurance System) and PALIS (Property and Liability Insurance System)—did not."

So much for IBM. We now know that one of Dad's focuses as the Safeco CTO (to use the modern term) was "fire and casualty" considerations.

I really can't think of anything much more boring than staid IBM coupled with an insurance company whose computer operations are run by the former Chief Auditor. That's about to change. At noon. In the University District of Seattle during the "beatnik" era.

Safeco's mainframes were, indeed, a big deal. Safeco had a large picture window on the ground floor facing the sidewalk where pedestrians walked by. Just inside the picture window was a mainframe computer with a front panel. The computer front panel had lots of blinky lights like in the movies. The featured mainframe was an RCA Spectra 70 (Figure 4.7), which was similar to, and mostly compatible with, the IBM System/360.

One of the Safeco staff figured out how to create an animation using the front panel blinky lights. It featured a dog and a fire hydrant. It ran during the lunch hour in the University district with countless thousands of pedestrians in the area. Fire and casualty indeed!

Figure 4.7. RCA Spectra 70 from 1965 sales brochure

---

[13] JoAnne Yates reports: https://phpa.me/hbc-beh-pdf

Dad merely put out the word that no such animations were to be repeated. No other action was taken.

It's weird how family disconnects happen. After the Safeco position, we moved to Los Angeles, then back to Washington State, but this time to Olympia. By the time I was walking past the Safeco Building to the Red Robin from the University of Washington, the Safeco Building didn't mean anything in particular. I knew about the dog and the fire hydrant but didn't connect it to the building I was walking past.

That's also the building where Dad stood in an interior doorway during either the Alaska earthquake (1964) or Seattle quake (1965). He watched the wall separate apart and come back together. We felt the Alaska quake (9.2 magnitude), 1600 miles away in Seattle, with about the same strength (as perceived by myself as a child) as the major Seattle quake (6.7 magnitude). The Alaska quake was a very big deal, the second most powerful ever recorded.

Seattle residents, thanks to that 1964 earthquake disaster, suddenly became very interested in "liquefaction." Like the damaged areas in Alaska, Seattle was built on reclaimed ground. Boeing proved out the concern with major damage from the Seattle quake. This is also why we don't see many large brick buildings in Seattle. They resist fire but quakes shake them to the ground. Wood structures, vulnerable to fire, withstand quakes quite well.

Fifteen years later, the Boeing Renton (Washington) plant, which had sustained major 1965 quake damage, would become the first aircraft company to receive a CRAY-1 supercomputer. That fact brings us back to two's complement arithmetic. Unlike Seymour Cray's CDC 6600 design which used ones' complement arithmetic, Seymour Cray's CRAY-1 used two's complement representation.

The primary difference between ones' complement and two's complement (besides where we place the apostrophe, before or after the "s") arithmetic is how we represent negative numbers.

- Ones' complement: Flip the bits
- Two's complement: Flip the bits and add one ("add" meaning arithmetic, as in "add one plus one")
- There is no "minus zero" with two's complement, which simplifies a lot of code

Here's an example calculation. Note the difference between ~2 (tilde-two) and -2 (minus-two):

```
0000 0010  Arithmetic 2
1111 1101  Ones' complement (~2)
1111 1110  Add 1 to form two's complement (-2)
```

On the first line, we have the number two in 8-bit binary representation. On the second line, we've flipped all the bits, moving from 2 to ~2. For the third line, we arithmetically add one, moving from ~2 to -2.

Here's the full pattern for negating two's complement numbers. These are the binary results we'd see when multiplying the number on the left by -1.

```
 1. Original value --> Negate the value
 2.
 3.     0  0000 0000     0  0000 0000
 4.     1  0000 0001    -1  1111 1111
 5.     2  0000 0010    -2  1111 1110
 6.   126  0111 1110  -126  1000 0010
 7.   127  0111 1111  -127  1000 0001
 8.  -128  1000 0000  -128  1000 0000 <-- weird
 9.  -127  1000 0001   127  0111 1111
10.  -126  1000 0010   126  0111 1110
11.    -2  1111 1110     2  0000 0010
12.    -1  1111 1111     1  0000 0001
13.     0  0000 0000     0  0000 0000
```

An 8-bit integer can take on 256 possible values. As an 8-bit unsigned integer, the 256 possible values are 0 through 255. As an 8-bit signed integer, the 256 possible values are -128 through 127. The maximum value is cut in half because one bit is used as the sign bit.

Larger-size integers will take on correspondingly larger ranges. A 16-bit unsigned integer has the range 0..65536 and the 16-bit signed integer has the range -32768..32767. These ranges will sound familiar if you use the MySQL data types[14] TINYINT (8-bit) and SMALLINT (16-bit).

In both PHP and C:

- Arithmetic operations use two's complement arithmetic
- Bitwise ("Boolean") operations use ones' complement bit manipulation

We're about to see both in the same calculation. Let's get back to our sample PHP code. Remember, the underlying operations, that is, the calculations we'll be making, would be the same in any C-like programming language.

---

[14] MySQL data types: https://phpa.me/mysql8-integer-types

The Calculation

Here is where left off:

```
$chunk = 0x51; // ASCII Q
$c = 1;        // Right hex digit
$b = 5;        // Left hex digit
```

Our next lines of code are:

```
$hex .= pack(
  'CC',
  (87 + $b + ((($b - 10) >> 8) & ~38)),
  (87 + $c + ((($c - 10) >> 8) & ~38))
);
```

Let's evaluate this the same way the computer would. We begin with the innermost set of parentheses, ($b - 10). We know $b has the value 5. (5 - 10) is -5. But what does -5 look like in binary? We'll form the two's complement of 5 by flipping the bits and adding one.

Let's "upgrade" our numbers from 8-bit values to 16-bit values. Our manipulations should be clearer when we're working with "wider" numbers.

```
0000 0000 0000 0101  5
1111 1111 1111 1010  ~5 (flip the bits)
                +1  Add one
------------------
1111 1111 1111 1011  -5 as two's complement
```

Our next step, same as the computer, is moving outward one set of parentheses:

```
(($b - 10) >> 8)
```

We know this reduces to:

```
((-5) >> 8)
```

Aha! We're doing a right shift. We know how to do a right shift. We know about sign propagation. We can do this!

```
1111 1111 1111 1011  -5
           >> 8  Shift 8 bits, extend sign bit from left
------------------
1111 1111 1111 1111  -1 (from table)
```

We know from the previous table that when a number is all zeroes (in binary), the number is 0, and when the number is all ones (in binary), and is treated as a two's complement number, that number is -1. A number consisting of all zeroes (in binary) is 0, and a number containing all ones is -1. That's actually good to know!

Moving out one more set of parentheses, we have:

```
((($b - 10) >> 8) & ~38)
```

Let's look at this the way the computer (compiler) might. We have the bitwise AND operator & with two operands, the left operand and the right operand. We just figured out the left operand `(($b - 10) >> 8)` evaluates to -1.

But, wait! We don't care it evaluates to -1. "Minus one" is a two's complement concept. The bitwise AND operator & requires ones' complement concepts. What matters to us now is that the left operand, in binary, is all ones. Let's keep going and this distinction will become more clear.

It's the same deal with the right operand, ~38. ~38 looks like a number, like -38 is a number, but it isn't. We're looking at the bitwise complement operator ~. This operator has one operand (not two operands like &), and that operand is whatever is to the right of the operator. We need to find the bitwise complement of (decimal) 38.

We know how to find a bitwise complement. We flip all the bits. All the bits that are 1 become 0 and all the bits that are 0 become 1. But how do we figure out what those bits are? That is, what is the binary representation of decimal 38?

We could:

- Convert decimal 38 to an octal or hexadecimal number, which then easily maps to binary, or
- Convert decimal 38 directly to binary

In all cases, we're working with powers of two. Hexadecimal works with powers of 16 which are themselves powers of two, and octal works with powers of eight which are also powers of two.

Let's convert to hexadecimal step by step.

1. Hexadecimal is base 16. 38 is more than 16. In fact, it's a bit more than 2*16 which is 32. Remember the 2, as in 2 times 16 is 32.
2. Find the remainder. 38 minus 32 is 6.
3. 38 is (2 * 16) plus 6. Our hexadecimal number is 0x26.

Now convert hexadecimal 0x26 to binary.

1. Hexadecimal 2 is binary 0010.

2. Hexadecimal 6 is binary 0110.

3. Therefore 0x26 is 0010 0110 (spaces added for clarity).

We know the above two facts (2 and 6 are 0010 and 0110 respectively) from the ASCII character set table. Let's determine the binary representation for ~38.

```
0000 0000 0010 0110   0x26 is 38 decimal
1111 1111 1101 1001   Ones' complement
```

At this point, we don't care what that result is as a decimal number. What we need is a binary value for the left operand and a binary value for the right operand. We now have both operands as binary numbers, so we can now perform the bitwise AND operation:

```
1111 1111 1111 1111   Left operand, (($b - 10) >> 8) result
1111 1111 1101 1001   Right operand, (~38) result
------------------    & (bitwise AND)
1111 1111 1101 1001
```

At this point we know the expression evaluates to 1111 1111 1101 1001. We're not much wiser—or are we? We can make a useful observation based on what just happened.

1. 1 ANDed with 0 is 0. 1 ANDed with 1 is 1. We know these two facts from the bitwise AND truth table.

2. The same holds true when the right side of the operation is a 1 rather than the left side: 0 ANDed with 1 is 0, and 1 ANDed with 1 is 1.

3. Therefore "anything" ANDed with 1 is the "anything", and 1 ANDed with "anything" is also the "anything", where "anything" is either 0 or 1.

4. Extending this to full computer words, the input value ANDed with all ones, or all ones ANDed with the input, produces a copy of the input value.

5. "All ones" can be represented as ~0 (ones' complement notation) or as -1 (two's complement notation); both produce the binary value containing all ones.

These facts give us some ways to think about our code:

• With a bitwise AND, we can swap the left and right sides and the result will be the same.

• Any value ANDed with -1 produces that same value.

In other words, when you do a bitwise AND with -1, the value doesn't change. That's like adding zero to a number (integer) or multiplying it by 1. None of these operations change the value.

What use is this fact? Remember our second line of code:

```
/** @var int $c */
$c = $chunk[1] & 0xf;
```

0xf, in 16-bit binary, is 0000 0000 0000 1111. Anything ANDed with zero will become zero. Anything ANDed with one will remain the same. The 0xf is a mask much like a stencil, allowing the rightmost four bits to pass through intact while clearing the upper bits to zero.

This is how we extract fields in a record, that is, how we extract specific bit ranges from a computer word. We set the mask to ones where we want to retain the information and the rest of the mask value, all zeroes, clears the extracted bits to zero.

The mask 0xf allows us to extract the rightmost four bits using a bitwise AND. The inverted mask ~0xf allows us to extract all bits except the bottom four bits.

This is rather tricky code. Let's review our steps, one set of parentheses at a time:

```
(87 + $b + ((($b - 10) >> 8)   & ~38)),
(87 + $b + (((5 - 10 ) >> 8)   & ~38)),
(87 + $b + (((-5      ) >> 8)  & ~38)),
(87 + $b + (((1111 1101) >> 8) & ~38)),
(87 + $b + ((1111 1111        ) & ~38)),
(87 + $b + (1111 1111 1101 1001     )),
```

Knowing the value of $b is 5, we can evaluate the left side:

```
(87 + $b + (1111 1111 1101 1001)),
(87 + 5  + (1111 1111 1101 1001)),
(92      + (1111 1111 1101 1001)),
```

We have a problem. The plus sign indicates we're doing an arithmetic operation rather than a bitwise operation. It's perfectly legal, though weird, to combine the two. We need to figure out the decimal value of 1111 1111 1101 1001 so we can add that to 92. We know the rule: Invert (flip the bits) and add one.

```
1111 1111 1101 1001  Value to convert
0000 0000 0010 0110  Flip the bits
                +1   Add one
-------------------
0000 0000 0010 0111  0x27 is 39 decimal
```

Since negating 1111 1111 1101 1001 produces 39 decimal, we know 1111 1111 1101 1001 is -39 decimal. Now we can complete our calculation:

```
(92      + (1111 1111 1101 1001)),
(92      + (-39                 )),
(92      +  -39                 ),
(53                             ),
```

As a quick review of how we got to 53:

1. Given that $b is 5, $b - 10 is -5.

2. -5 shifted right 8 bits is -1 thanks to sign propagation on right shift.

3. ~38 is -39.

4. -1 (which is all ones) AND "anything" is "anything": -1 & -39 is -39.

5. 87 + 5 + -39 is 53.

So what is the point of all this? Our code reads:

```
$hex .= pack(
  'CC',
  (87 + $b + ((($b - 10) >> 8) & ~38)),
  (87 + $c + ((($c - 10) >> 8) & ~38))
);
```

*   We are encoding ASCII "Q" as a string of hexadecimal digits.

*   "Q" is hexadecimal 51 (0x51).

*   By a remarkable and happy coincidence, ASCII "5" is represented by decimal 53.

What have we done? We've converted the left digit of 0x51 to its ASCII equivalent. That's the first complex expression in the above code.

Now we can fast-forward. The two complex expressions are identical to each other except the first one uses the variable $b (whose value is 5) and the second one uses the variable $c (whose value is 1). We extracted the two hexadecimal digits 5 and 1 into these two variables.

If we do the second calculation, it's a fair guess that when we use 1 as input rather than 5, our result will be a proportionally smaller number, namely 49. Sure enough, ASCII "1" is represented by decimal 49.

Our complex code now reduces to:

```
$hex .= pack('CC', 53, 49);
$hex === '51'; // ASCII Q is 0x51
```

Here is the code we worked through annotated with our calculations:

```
1.  $hex = '';
2.  $len = Binary::safeStrlen($binString); // 1
3.  for ($i = 0; $i < $len; ++$i) { // Straight-line code
4.     $chunk = \unpack('C', Binary::safeSubstr($binString, $i, 1));
5.                        // $chunk[1] = 0x51;
6.     $c = $chunk[1] & 0xf; // 1
7.     $b = $chunk[1] >> 4;  // 5
8.
9.     $hex .= pack(
10.       'CC',
11.       (87 + $b + ((($b - 10) >> 8) & ~38)), // 53
12.       (87 + $c + ((($c - 10) >> 8) & ~38))  // 49
13.    );
14. }
15. return $hex; // return string '51';
```

Learning

We worked our way through a complex piece of software, even though it was a very few lines of code. We walked through the code as a computer would, step by excruciating step.

What's the important skill here? It's not the binary arithmetic. It's not hidden in ones' complement or two's complement notation; it's not the shifting and masking. Those are all good to know, but none of those are the crucial skill here.

The important skill is what we just demonstrated and practiced. It's the ability to walk through the code as a computer would, step by excruciating step. This is how we find the off-by-one errors, the unexpected type conversions, the edge cases. This is how we reconstruct the series of events leading to the observed result.

There's a vast difference between looking at a piece of software and telling yourself, "I think I see what this does," and actually walking through each step.

Is it necessary to walk through every bit of software, doing every calculation by hand? Certainly not! What's important is to understand the flow. Identify with the computer's perspective on that piece of software. Sometimes it does take a session of walking through by hand. When that time comes, you'll know what to do!

Summary

Here's what we learned:

- The bitwise operators (by whatever name) work with *ones' complement* representation.

- The arithmetic operators (integer arithmetic) work with *two's complement* representation.

- It's perfectly valid (but weird) to combine the two types of operators in a single expression—it pays to know what you're looking at.

Chapter

5

Design an Algorithm in Your Head

If you have trouble making change for a dollar without a calculator, and don't care, this chapter may not be for you. Otherwise, come along with me! We'll be converting between numbering systems. We'll create an algorithm for converting between decimal (integer) and hexadecimal numbers.

Donald Knuth

We convert between different units of measure all the time. We convert between days and weeks, hours and minutes. How long are two 90-minute blocks? Three hours. We do the same with pounds, ounces, fluid ounces, and quarts—or with the far more sane metric units.

We will begin by converting between different units of measure (seconds, minutes, hours, etc.). Then, we'll take on a more exotic task: converting between different numbering systems.

What is a "numbering system?" This is one of those terms that is difficult to define but easy to explain by example. "Base 10" is our standard decimal numbering system. "Base 16" is hexadecimal, and so on. The "base" of the numbering system is also called the "radix."

The Art of Computer Programming, Volume 2: Seminumerical Algorithms (Third Edition) By Donald E. Knuth (1998) introduces "Radix Conversion" (page 319):

> *If our ancestors had invented arithmetic by counting with their two fists or their eight fingers, instead of their ten "digits," we would never have to worry about writing binary-decimal conversion routines. (And we would perhaps never have learned as much about number systems.)*

What is an algorithm? Or, more importantly, why do we care? To get there, I need to explain another term whose meaning has changed.

A half-century ago we were called "computer programmers." What we now call software development, or software engineering was, back then, computer programming. There are countless arguments online about differences in meaning for these terms. But 50 years ago, we were all "computer programmers" because we programmed (digital or analog) computers.

Eight years earlier, young Donald Knuth[1] "received his bachelor of science degree, simultaneously being given a master of science degree by a special award of the faculty who considered his work exceptionally outstanding." Three years later he was Dr. Knuth with a Ph.D. in mathematics from CalTech and joined CalTech's faculty.

Knuth wrote the classic work *The Art of Computer Programming*[2] (originally three volumes, 1968-73). Note that a *Professor of Mathematics* is calling what we do an *art*. What does our "art" consist of?

---

[1]   *Donald Knuth:* https://en.wikipedia.org/wiki/Donald_Knuth
[2]   *The Art of Computer Programming:* https://phpa.me/wikip-art-programming

- Fundamental Algorithms
- Seminumerical Algorithms
- Searching and Sorting (Algorithms)

In short, the art of programming computers is, and always has been, the art of creating and implementing algorithms.

> *An Algorithm[3] is a step-by-step procedure for solving a problem or accomplishing some end, especially by a computer.*

Algorithms are so common that we often see them as libraries or packages. For example, `sort()` implements various sorting algorithms.

You have likely solved various business problems by creating algorithms. You may have automated parts of a manual procedure. When you identified the specific steps to automate, you identified (or created) an algorithm.

Conversion

Let's begin with the arbitrary integer 227,301 (my car's mileage). How might we figure out (without a calculator) how many days (or weeks) are in 227,301 seconds? Well, how many seconds are in a day? A week?

Let's figure this out.

- 60 seconds are in a minute.
- 60 minutes are in an hour. Therefore `60*60`, or 3,600, seconds are in an hour.
- 24 hours are in a day. Therefore `3600*24`, or 86,400 seconds are in a day.
- Seven days are in a week. Therefore `86400*7`, or 604,800 seconds are in a week.

We have now bracketed our target number. We know 227,301 seconds is more than one day but less than one week.

Remember, we're going as far as we can without a calculator. That's rough! But we can do it. Our question is, how many units of 86,400 seconds are in 227,301 seconds? That is, how many whole days are in 227,301 seconds?

Let's reduce this to more manageable numbers. Divide both numbers by a thousand. Now, how many times does 8.6 divide into 22.7? Think about it this way:

---

[3]   Algorithm: *https://phpa.me/mw-algorithm*

- We know eight (that's 8.6 rounded down) times two is 16 (smaller than 22.7), whereas eight times three is 24 (larger than 22.7).

- We also know nine (that's 8.6 rounded up) times two is 18 (smaller than 22.7), whereas nine times three is 27 (larger than 22.7).

Do you see our reasoning here? We reduced everything to single-digit multiplication so we can do it in our head. We now know for certain that 227,301 seconds is more than 2 full days but less than 3 days.

How many seconds are in two days? That would be 86,400 times two. You can double a number in your head, right? 86 multiplied by two is 172, and 400 multiplied by two is 800. The answer is 172,800.

How many seconds are left over? Subtract 172,800 from 227,301:

```
  227,301
 -172,800
 ========
   54,501
```

Next, we ask how many hours are in 54,501 seconds? Divide both sides by a thousand as before, so we can estimate the number of hours in our head.

> We will be using a very similar thought process in converting decimal numbers to hexadecimal numbers. You may be surprised. We're working from the known or familiar (days, hours, weeks) to the less familiar (hexadecimal by hand).

How many times does 3.6 divide into 54.5? 3.6 comes from the fact that we have 3,600 seconds in an hour. Rounding down, we know that three times 18 is 54 (less than 54.5). Rounding up, we see four multiplied by 13 is 52 (less than 54.5) Since 15 is roughly halfway between 13 and 18, let's estimate that 54,501 seconds contains 15 hours.

I have trouble with the mental calculation of three times 18. I can do single-digit multiplication in my head, but double-digit multiplication, such as multiplying 18, is not so easy for me. I have a couple of options for juggling the numbers to make it easier for me to do in my head:

- Cut 18 in half and double the result. Half of 18 is 9. I can do that much in my head easily enough. Three times 9 is 27. Double 27 to get 54, the final answer. It's much easier for me to take several steps to get at the answer, than laboriously figure out three times 18.

- Double one of the numbers and cut the other in half to arrive at the same result. Three times 18 becomes six times 9, which I know is 54.

In short, I know my own limitations. If I can reduce the problem to single-digit calculations, I can do it in my head. As you become more aware of your own capabilities and limitations, through practice and more practice, you'll be able to develop your own strategy for just about anything. Meanwhile, though, we'll continue to work with *my* limitations for our example!

We estimated that 54,501 seconds contains 15 hours. 3,600 seconds (per hour) times 15 (estimated number of hours) equals 54,000. We made a perfect estimate! If you're not sure how we got here, please take another look at the thought process. We reduced the problem to single-digit numbers so we could do this in our head. It's a useful habit to form!

54,501 minus 54,000 equals 501 seconds. This tells us 227,301 seconds equals two days, 15 hours, and 501 seconds.

How many minutes are in 501 seconds? We have 60 seconds in a minute. Divide both sides by 10 to give us single-digit numbers once again. We now ask, how many times does six go into 50.1? We know six multiplied by eight is 48, so 60 times eight is 480.

501 seconds minus 480 seconds (which is eight minutes) leaves 21 seconds. Therefore 227,301 seconds equals two days, 15 hours, 8 minutes, 21 seconds.

If we then implement this in PHP, we'd get something like Listing 5.1. I'll leave implementing this using recursion as an exercise for you.

Listing 5.1. Seconds Converter

```
1.  <?php
2.
3.  namespace Ewbarnard\Algorithm;
4.
5.  class SecondsConverter
6.  {
7.      public const KEY_WEEKS = 'weeks';
8.      public const KEY_DAYS = 'days';
9.      public const KEY_HOURS = 'hours';
10.     public const KEY_MINUTES = 'minutes';
11.     public const KEY_SECONDS = 'seconds';
12.
```

```
13.    private const SECONDS_TO_MINUTES = 60;
14.    private const SECONDS_TO_HOURS = 60 * 60;
15.    private const SECONDS_TO_DAYS = 60 * 60 * 24;
16.    private const SECONDS_TO_WEEKS = 60 * 60 * 24 * 7;
17.
18.    private $result;
19.
20.    public function convert(int $seconds) : array {
21.        $this->result = [];
22.
23.        $seconds = $this->reduce(
24.            $seconds, self::SECONDS_TO_WEEKS, self::KEY_WEEKS
25.        );
26.        $seconds = $this->reduce(
27.            $seconds, self::SECONDS_TO_DAYS, self::KEY_DAYS
28.        );
29.        $seconds = $this->reduce(
30.            $seconds, self::SECONDS_TO_HOURS, self::KEY_HOURS
31.        );
32.        $seconds = $this->reduce(
33.            $seconds, self::SECONDS_TO_MINUTES, self::KEY_MINUTES
34.        );
35.
36.        $this->result[self::KEY_SECONDS] = $seconds;
37.        return $this->result;
38.    }
39.
40.    private function reduce(int $seconds, int $multiple, string $key) : int {
41.        if ($seconds >= $multiple) {
42.            $this->result[$key] = (int)floor($seconds / $multiple);
43.            $seconds %= $multiple;
44.        }
45.        return $seconds;
46.    }
47. }
```

We can use our converter as follows. See Listing 5.2.

Listing 5.2. Run seconds converter

```php
 1. <?php
 2.
 3. use Ewbarnard\Algorithm\SecondsConverter;
 4.
 5. require_once 'SecondsConverter.php';
 6.
 7. $converter = new SecondsConverter();
 8. $result = $converter->convert(227301);
 9. echo '<?php' . PHP_EOL . '$result = ' .
10.     var_export($result, true) . ';' . PHP_EOL;
```

The resulting output is Output 5.1.

Output 5.1. Seconds converter output

```php
<?php
$result = array (
   'days' => 2,
   'hours' => 15,
   'minutes' => 8,
   'seconds' => 21,
);
```

Algorithm

An algorithm[4] is simply a set of rules for solving a problem or class of problems. Could we write down a general procedure (that is, an algorithm) for doing what we just did? Certainly!

1. List the available units of measure. We are using seconds, minutes, hours, days, weeks; with the input value being in seconds.

2. Determine the largest unit smaller than the input value. 227,301 seconds is larger than one day but smaller than one week.

3. Determine the number of whole units larger than the input value. Two days.

4. Subtract off the whole units, expressed in the input value's units. 227,301 minus 172,800 leaves 54,501.

5. Repeat the above steps for each such residual value, ending when reduced to the input

---

[4]   algorithm: https://en.wikipedia.org/wiki/Algorithm

value's units. Determine 15 hours, 8 minutes, leaving 21 seconds.

Certainly, there are more proper ways to declare our algorithm. Note what we did.

1.   We worked through an example by hand.
2.   We wrote a generalized set of rules for accomplishing that task.
3.   We could then write software implementing that set of rules. We chose a PHP implementation.

Furthermore, along the way, we got better at working through some calculations in our head!

Decimal to Hexadecimal

We took 227,301 and worked through our crazy calendar system, converting to days, hours, minutes, and seconds. Now we're going to interpret 227,301 as a decimal number (an integer) and convert it to hexadecimal notation. Would you believe we can use the same algorithm? Let's give it a try.

In decimal notation, instead of (seconds, minutes, hours, days, weeks) we have (ones, tens, hundreds, thousands, ten-thousands). In hexadecimal we have:

- The right-most digit is the one's[5] or units column. (0x1 is decimal 1)
- The next (second from the right) is the ten's column. It contains 16 units per digit. (0x10 is decimal 16)
- The third digit from the right is the hundred's column. 16*16 equals 256. (0x100 is decimal 256)
- The fourth digit from the right is the thousand's column. 256*16 equals 4,096. (0x1000 is decimal 4,096)
- The fifth digit is the ten-thousand's column. 4,096*16 equals 65,536. (0x10000 is decimal 65,536)
- The sixth digit is the hundred-thousand's column. 65,536*16 equals 1,048,576. (0x100000 is 1,048,576)

We now have the information we need to run our algorithm. 227,301 is greater than 65,536 and less than 1,048,576.

How many times does 65,536 divide into 227,301? Instead ask, how many times does 6.5 divide into 22.7? Six times three (rounding down) is 18; seven times three (rounding up) is

---

[5]   one's: https://phpa.me/wyzant-place-value

21. Both are slightly less than 22.7, so let's estimate that 65,536 divides into 227,301 three times.

Three times 65,536 is 196,608. Do the subtraction to find the remainder:

```
  227,301
 -196,608
 ========
   30,693
```

We now have one hexadecimal digit, 0x30000, and the decimal left-over of 30693. Our next unit is 4,096. How many times does 4,096 divide into 30,693? Well, how many times does 4.1 divide into 30.7? Four times seven is 28, so we'll use seven as our estimate. 4,096*7 equals 28,672. As before, subtract to find the residue:

```
  30,693
 -28,672
 =======
   2,021
```

We now have two hexadecimal digits, 0x37000, with decimal residue 2,021.

Our next unit is 256. Since we know our powers of two, we immediately note 256*8 equals 2,048. That's slightly above 2,021, so our estimate is seven. 256*7 equals 1,792.

Here's how I do the subtraction in my head. 1,792 is eight short of 1,800. 2,021 minus 1,800 is 221. Add in the other eight to get 229. That is, 2,021 minus 1,792 is 229.

> *It does not matter how you make your estimate, so long as you come up with the correct number. I'm showing you my thought process in creating the estimate. Your thought process could be entirely different but equally correct and likely faster.*

We now have 0x37700 with residue 229. How many times does 16 divide into 229? Note that 229 is close to 256, and we know 16*16 is 256. It's short of 256 by 27. That means our estimate is 14. 16*14 equals 224.

Therefore our fourth digit is 14 with residue five because 229 minus 224 equals five. The hexadecimal digits are zero through nine, then a through f. Ten is "a," eleven is "b," and so on through fifteen being "f." Fourteen is "e." We, therefore, have 0x377e0 with residue five.

Our final answer? Hexadecimal 0x377e5 equals decimal 227,301.

Hexadecimal to Decimal

Converting to decimal is simple—and quick. We do plain addition with decimal arithmetic.

To convert hexadecimal 377e5 to decimal, add the digits. We'll calculate left-to-right, but you could certainly calculate right-to-left:

- Three multiplied by 65,536 equals 196,608

- Seven multiplied by 4,096 equals 28,672

- Seven times 256 equals 1,792

- E multiplied by 16 equals 224

- Five multiplied by one equals 5

Add up the numbers:

```
    196,608
+    28,672
+     1,792
+       224
+         5
- - - - - - - - -
    227,301
```

Could you write down an algorithm for converting from hexadecimal to decimal notation, assuming whole non-negative numbers? I bet you could! Do you also see by working through the problem once, with a concrete example, it's easier to visualize and create the algorithm?

Base 62

You may have encountered Base64[6] encoding. It's a way of transmitting binary data across the internet using "safe" printable characters. These are ASCII characters, predating Unicode. One of several problems with the encoding scheme is that different implementations use different sets of characters.

Most schemes use:

- The decimal digits 0..9

- The lower-case English alphabetic letters a..z

---

[6]   Base64: https://en.wikipedia.org/wiki/Base64

- The upper-case English alphabetic letters A..Z

If you're good with arithmetic, and you surely are by this point, you'll have noted that we have a set of 62 characters. We need a total of 64, so we need to add two more characters. Therein lays the problem. The Wikipedia article includes a table with more than a dozen encoding variants.

What if we encoded using only the above 62 characters? We will have solved most of the problems requiring those variants. We don't expect anyone else to adopt our "Base 62" algorithm. We're merely creating a Proof of Concept.

You will have guessed that we already know how to convert an integer to Base 62. It's just like base 16 (hexadecimal) except that we have more characters to work with.

Here are the encoder and decoder. See Listing 5.3.

Listing 5.3. Base 62 Encoder

```php
1. <?php
2.
3. namespace Ewbarnard\Algorithm;
4.
5. class Base62
6. {
7.     private const BASE62 =
8.         '0123456789aAbBcCdDeEfFgGhHiIjJkKlLmMnNoOpPqQrRsStTuUvVwWxXyYzZ';
9.
10.    //private const BASE62 = '0123456789abcdef';
11.
12.    public static function encode(int $basis) : string {
13.        $base62 = str_split(self::BASE62);
14.        $modulus = count($base62);
15.        $encoded = '';
16.
17.        while ($basis) {
18.            $offset = $basis % $modulus;
19.            $encoded = $base62[$offset] . $encoded;
20.            $basis -= $offset;
21.            $basis /= $modulus;
22.        }
23.
24.        return $encoded;
25.    }
26.
```

```
27.    public static function decode(string $encoded) : int {
28.        $base62 = str_split(self::BASE62);
29.        $map = array_flip($base62);
30.        $modulus = count($map);
31.        $characters = array_reverse(str_split($encoded));
32.        $basis = 0;
33.        $times = 1;
34.
35.        foreach ($characters as $character) {
36.            $digit = $map[$character];
37.            $basis += ($digit * $times);
38.            $times *= $modulus;
39.        }
40.
41.        return $basis;
42.    }
43. }
```

We can test our encoder/decoder as follows. See Listing 5.4. When we encode our integer 227,301, we should be able to decode the result and arrive back at our original number.

Listing 5.4. Run encoder/decoder

```
1. <?php
2.
3. use Ewbarnard\Algorithm\Base62;
4.
5. require_once 'Base62.php';
6. $before = 227301;
7. $encoded = Base62::encode($before);
8. $after = Base62::decode($encoded);
9. echo "Before: $before" . PHP_EOL .
10.     "Encoded: $encoded" . PHP_EOL .
11.     "After: $after" . PHP_EOL;
```

The resulting output is Output 5.2.

Output 5.2. Encoder/decoder output

```
Before: 227301
Encoded: Y89
After: 227301
```

So far so good. Now let's make this interesting. The encoder/decoder uses constant BASE62 as the list of characters available for encoding. Let's change that list to the sixteen hexadecimal characters and see what happens:

```
private const BASE62 = '0123456789abcdef';
```

Running the same test, using the same integer 227,301 as input, our result becomes Output 5.3.

Output 5.3. Hexadecimal converter output

```
Before: 227301
Encoded: 377e5
After: 227301
```

How about that? By changing our list of available characters for encoding, we created a decimal-to-hexadecimal converter along with the matching decimal-to-hexadecimal converter. We know it's correct because we first did the calculation by hand.

If we tear the encoder/decoder apart, we'll see it indeed does implement the algorithm we worked out by hand. If this were to become production code, we'd want to check for integer overflow and invalid input.

Summary

We took on a probably-unfamiliar problem, namely converting from decimal to hexa-decimal by hand. We first worked with a familiar example and then created a set of rules for performing the task.

It's often easiest to work from the known to the unknown. Our problem is in converting from one set of units (decimal or base 10) to another set of units (hexadecimal, base 16). We're all familiar with converting between minutes, hours, days, and so on… so we initially created our algorithm using that familiar territory.

We discovered that we actually created a general-purpose algorithm for converting from one set of units to another, and back again. We used the *same* algorithm for converting from decimal to hexadecimal.

We proved this out by creating a Base 62 encoder/decoder using the same algorithm. When we changed from 62 characters down to 16 characters without changing anything else, sure enough, we found we have a hexadecimal encoder/decoder.

We created something that actually works. That's another achievement unlocked!

Chapter

6

Abstract Thinking

Software is built of abstractions layered on top of more abstractions. We, therefore, all do abstract thinking one way or another. But there is one form of abstract thinking which can help us to understand—and communicate—how the whole system works. We'll use the flow of a river as an analogy to help communicate that type of understanding.

6. Abstract Thinking

Sometimes, we can't just "read the code" to see how something works. The code is there and available to be read, but it doesn't provide the whole story. We can read the code implementing a specific object, for instance, but it doesn't show us the impact to a system creating thousands of objects per second.

In effect, sometimes we can't see the forest for the trees. When we "read the code" we're looking at one individual tree, so to speak, rather than the living, changing, forest as a whole. In this situation, a particular type of abstract thinking comes into play.

It can be remarkably challenging to think in the abstract even though we do it all the time. The Learning Mind website[1] describes abstract thinking—and describes what we do every day:

> *Abstract thinking is the ability to think about things that are not actually present. People who think in the abstract way look at the broader significance of ideas and information rather than the concrete details. Abstract thinkers are interested in the deeper meaning of things and the bigger picture.*
>
> *Perhaps the easiest way to explain abstract thinking is to compare it with its opposite— concrete reasoning. Concrete thinkers are more comfortable with what exists right now. They like things that are clear and tangible and that they can hold in their hands. Concrete thinkers like to follow instructions and have detailed plans. They hate anything that is fuzzy or ambiguous. They do not usually "read between the lines."*

The above article explains we all use both types of thinking, but, "for most people, one type of thinking dominates." In our software development realm, I think of the above definition as the difference between design and implementation. To put it another way, as "concepts" versus "code." When we think in concepts we transcend varying computer languages; when we think in code we're implementing a concept in a specific language (or group of languages).

This chapter looks at a different type of abstract thinking. It's where the code is there to be read and understood as part of an existing (concrete) system, but the code doesn't tell the story. We'll be looking at the situation where one entity is producing messages (tasks to perform) and another entity is consuming those messages (performing the tasks).

This situation is the producer-consumer pattern. When we look at producing and consuming individual messages, we can read the code and see how it works. Computer science courses[2] generally take this individual-message view:

---

[1]   Learning Mind website: https://learning-mind.com/abstract-thinking/
[2]   Computer science courses: https://phpa.me/lecture-18-concurrency

> *A classic concurrent programming design pattern is producer-consumer, where we designate processes as either producers or consumers. The producers are responsible for adding to some shared data structure. The consumers are responsible for removing from that structure. Only one party, either a single producer or a single consumer, can access the structure at any given time.*

Patterns

However, the producer-consumer pattern can take us well beyond the concurrent-access issues described above. With a busy website, for example, we could have thousands of clients (users) simultaneously requesting webpages and multiple servers simultaneously (or nearly simultaneously) fulfilling those requests with few concurrency issues.

We're now thinking of the already-abstract pattern "in the abstract" and using it to describe more situations. This, again, is something we do all the time. All software is basically abstractions layered on top of abstractions.

We're considering a different way of looking at software. Why? So we can:

- Better understand the system we're working with, and
- Better communicate that understanding with other people.

The key, as with all software development, is the latter part. Martin Fowler explains, in *Patterns of Enterprise Application Architecture* (2003), p. 10:

> *For an experienced designer, the value of the pattern is not that it gives you a new idea; the value lies in helping you communicate your idea.*

Of course, the latter part—communicating—depends on understanding the system in the first place. Let's use the producer-consumer pattern as our example to show you what I mean.

Data Flow

In the chapter *Think Like a Computer*, we learned a certain way of thinking about our software:

> *What's the big secret? It's thinking about software in terms of flow rather than the result. I don't mean the flow of data through a system; I mean the flow of the processor (CPU and friends) executing your instructions (the software).*

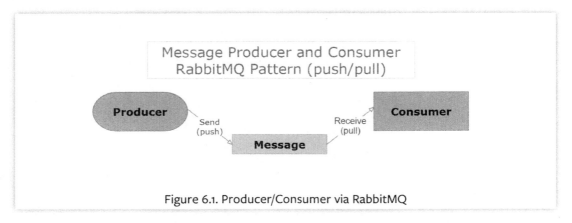

Figure 6.1. Producer/Consumer via RabbitMQ

Now we are looking at the flow of data through a system. I don't mean the typical flow of data between database and webpage. I mean the things that propagate through a software system such as request and response.

For example, we might have a situation where file uploads require additional processing. Video uploads, for example, might require resampling, conversion to different formats, and generating thumbnail images. We could accomplish this by sending a message through a work queue requesting the offline (asynchronous) processing (Figure 6.1). The "producer" defines the work to be performed, creates a message, and sends the message to a message queue. The "consumer" registers with the message queue and asks for the next available message from the queue. So far, so good.

It's easy to visualize a *single* request. When we look at the code generating the message (the message producer) or the code processing the video file (the message consumer, also called the worker), we're studying how we handle a single request.

Figure 6.1 also shows a *push* model between the producer and the message queue. The producer chooses to send the message, that is, it is *pushing* the message. If something had requested the message, that would be a *pull* model, where something is "pulling" the message from the producer.

The consumer, on the other hand, registers with the queue and requests the next available message. Thus the consumer is pulling the message. The "push" and "pull" descriptions tell us who or what caused the action to take place.

This particular approach is designed to scale as needed. For example, thousands of web requests might all simultaneously generate messages and place them in the queue. We might have a single worker handling messages in sequence, or we might have multiple workers working in parallel. Either way, we have a flow of messages from producer to consumer.

The consumer has offloaded work from the producer, allowing the producer to be more responsive by not waiting for the extra work to complete.

Analogies can help communicate concepts or describe a system. I like to describe message flow as being like a river, since most people are familiar with rivers. Figure 6.2 is the Cascade River flowing into Lake Superior. We can, for example, note the brown streaks in the river. The brown is organic material from bogs upriver and helps us visualize the routes. The ice-coated rocks show us the cascade generates water spray.

Data flows have bottlenecks. Again, the river analogy can help communicate this concept. We might use the waterfall photo to explain that by tuning one area, we can improve overall throughput. There are many times that different analogies can help communication.

Figure 6.2. Cascade River

This particular photo points out another critical analogy. Everything flows from upstream to downstream. That makes sense, right? If you're building a messaging system, go with the flow; work from upstream to downstream. Many systems are designed around this principle—messages and data flow from upstream to downstream. If you want to understand the system, find and follow that flow.

Cryptonomicon portrays the fictional Lawrence Waterhouse arriving at Bletchley Park to observe how German communications (Enigma messages) are being decrypted during World War II (pp. 244-247):

> *"Right. Well, what would you like to see?"*
>
> *"I'm trying to get an overall sense of how the information flows."*
>
> *"Well, we are close to the beginnings of it here—these are the headwaters. Our well-springs are the Y service—military and amateur radio operators who listen in on Jerry's radio transmissions, and provide us with these." Packard takes a slip from a motorcyclist's*

pannier and hands it to Waterhouse. "This one came in from one of our stations in Kent,"
Packard says. "It is a Chaffinch message."

"So—one of Rommel's?"

"Yes. This intercept came from Cairo. Chaffinch gets top priority, which is why this
message is on top of the pile."

Packard steps over to a small wooden hatch set low into one of the hut's exterior walls.
Next to it sits an office tray with a cup hook screwed into each end, and a string tied to
each cup hook. One of the strings is piled up loose on the floor. The wall hatch has been slid
shut on the other string. Packard puts the message slip on top of a pile of similar ones that
has accumulated in the tray, then slides the hatch open, revealing a narrow tunnel leading
away from the hut.

"Okay, your pull!" he shouts.

"Okay, my pull!" comes an answering voice a moment later. The string goes taut and the
tray slides into the tunnel and disappears.

"On its way to Hut 3," Packard explains.

"Then so am I," Waterhouse says.

However, there's another way to visualize the situation. How might we visualize the
flow, but from the perspective of the message flowing down the river? Figure 6.3 illustrates

Figure 6.3. Voyageurs Shooting the Rapids

voyageurs shooting the rapids. If you can picture traveling in that boat, you can picture the journey from the voyageur's perspective. Tolkien's *The Fellowship of the Ring* describes the party's journey down the River Anduin. Is it possible, then, to visualize the data flow from the perspective of an individual message or packet? Certainly!

Now that we understand the flow, it's time to consider specific implementation patterns. This is where our pristine flow becomes muddy, so to speak.

Producer and Consumer

We talked about "producer" and "consumer" with the idea the producer passes an actual message to the consumer. Are there different ways to think about this? Yes. Figure 6.4 shows a web server request where we are *receiving* data rather than *sending* data. With a RESTful API, this would be a GET rather than POST, PUT, or PATCH.

Note that with a POST rather than GET we reverse the roles (Figure 6.5). The client becomes the producer rather than consumer, and the server becomes the consumer.

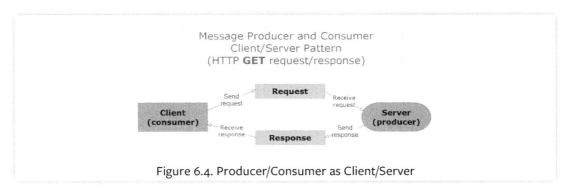

Figure 6.4. Producer/Consumer as Client/Server

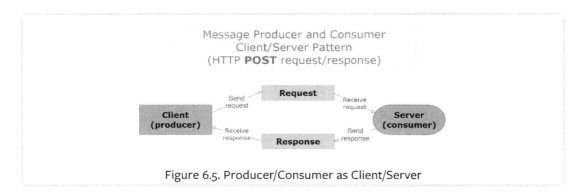

Figure 6.5. Producer/Consumer as Client/Server

This is a bit weird. We usually think of the client as originating the request and the server as responding. That part remains true. But now we're thinking about the flow of data and realizing it's a different situation. When the client requests a webpage, image, or whatever, it's *consuming* the response, and the server is *producing* the response. On the other hand, when we create a new record, such as by submitting web form data, the client is *producing* the record, and the server is *consuming* the record. In terms of data flow, the data of interest could be flowing:

- inbound to the server with the request,
- outbound from the server with the response,
- or both.

Does the river analogy still hold? Yes, even though it might be a bit harder to visualize. We can look at the code implementing an individual request and response, but we also know that's not the full story. It's not the individual server request that matters; it's the requests in the aggregate. If you can visualize that as a flow or a pipeline, great.

What happens with a traffic spike? Sometimes the master database, or some other single point of failure, becomes the bottleneck. If you can picture an actual physical log jam (Figure 6.6), it becomes easier to understand and communicate the problem and nature of the necessary solution.

Figure 6.6. Log jam

Observer

We could implement both the messaging pattern (Figure 6.1) and client/server patterns (Figure 6.4 and Figure 6.5) without the intermediary. Where both producer and consumer are on the same server, we could have the one entity call the other entity directly, passing any message or another payload back and forth. The inline call ensures synchronous processing. At this point, the "river" analogy becomes muddy because everything is now part of the same process. The flow is still there but harder to separately identify. Furthermore, if you recognize that the flow is still there, even though unseen, it remains easier to understand and study the system as a whole.

The observer pattern[3] usually works inline, which makes it difficult to perceive.

> *The observer pattern is a software design pattern in which an object, called the subject, maintains a list of its dependents, called observers, and notifies them automatically of any state changes, usually by calling one of their methods. It is mainly used to implement distributed event handling systems.*

We often have "observers" or "event listeners" in PHP frameworks. I find them difficult to work with because they're invisible. For example, WordPress has filters and actions; Drupal uses hooks and events; CakePHP has an event system; Magento registers observers.

All of these examples provide ways for custom solutions in specific applications. When an event happens, such as successfully reading a row from a database, the event information is passed to any functions listening for it. The whole process is invisible because the whole thing is (intentionally) hidden from sight. It's this lack of visibility which makes debugging far more difficult.

To use our river analogy, observers usually operate synchronously, in place. (Figure 6.7 shows workers amid the log jam, freeing up individual logs. They are literally doing their own thing as they see fit.) When the event happens, the listeners are immediately executed, one after another, before processing continues. Your data, message, or database might spontaneously change between one line of code and the next without there being any apparent reason. It might be that there was an observer that did something.

The observer pattern does have another form. Rather than working invisibly inline, it can follow the "pub-sub" (publish/subscribe) model. Rather than the event trigger running through a list of listeners (observers), the event trigger sends (publishes) the event

---

[3]   *observer pattern: https://phpa.me/wikip-observer-pattern*

Figure 6.7. Log jam

information to a message queue, much like Figure 6.1. Observers subscribe to the queue. Thus, the observer is working asynchronously rather than synchronously.

The whole point of the observer pattern is the mainline code does not need to be responsible for knowing anything about the observers. For example, there might be a website with people who want to know about blog updates. So long as there is a list of observers, any blog update can cause that list of people to be notified, without the author being conscious of who is on that list.

Summary

There's an old joke that runs like this:

> *We just got a new project. You three start coding while I find out the requirements.*

At some point, the project gets large enough that "reading the code" isn't enough. We need to think about the system as a whole. We must consider how the components fit together, but we also need to look at more than merely the system at rest. We need to think about flows, influences, spikes, emergencies, aberrations. We need to communicate concepts and describe implications.

We need to do a lot of this thinking before writing a single line of production code. It's not just that we shouldn't start coding before we know the requirements. We need to understand the system as a whole, and the flow *through* that system so we can fit those requirements into the "big picture."

Software rarely gets built in a vacuum. As we consider the big picture, we need to communicate our insights. Describing actual rivers with cascades and log jams can help create that shared vision of the system.

Chapter

7

Turtles All the Way Down

It's time to take on one more component of the hardware/software ecosystem: a compiler. The PHP compiler is written in C. In this chapter, we learn how to navigate the codebase using the source browser and search capability. We'll see various resources and techniques for learning the codebase. We'll walk through the `strpos` function's source code as a specific example.

Turtles

The expression Turtles all the way down[1] describes the mythological idea of a World Turtle that supports the earth on its back. See Figure 7.1.

This brings up the question: What supports the World Turtle? The answer is that it rests upon another turtle.

That brings out the next question: What supports the turtle supporting the World Turtle? The answer is that it's turtles all the way down.

Meanwhile, the PHP language's mascot is the "elePHPant." That fact reminds me of the expression "an elephant is a horse designed by committee." PHP does contain a wonderful collection of inconsistencies; however, since the release of PHP 7, PHP has been rapidly maturing as a programming language.

The Popular Science Monthly magazine (Volume X) of March 1877 contains the article *How the earth was regarded in old times*[2] beginning on page 542 ("Hindu" is spelled "Hindoo" in the original text.) See Figure 7.2.

> *The Hindoos held the earth to be hemispherical, and to be supported like a boat turned upside down upon the heads of four elephants, which stood on the back of an immense*

Figure 7.1. Stacked Turtles

FIG. 4.—THE HINDOO EARTH.

Figure 7.2. The Hindoo Earth

---

[1] *Turtles all the way down:*
     https://phpa.me/turtles-way-down
[2] *How the earth was regarded in old times:*
     https://phpa.me/popsci-542

tortoise. It is usually said that the tortoise rested on nothing, but the Hindoos main-tained that it floated on the surface of the universal ocean. The learned Hindoos, however, say that these animals were merely symbolical, the four elephants meaning the four directions of the compass, and the tortoise meaning eternity.

This story reminds me of Parisa Tabriz explaining "how computers and software work" in *So you want to work in security?*[3]

Much of applied computer science is about solving problems with layers of abstrac-tion…

When I think of computer science as layer upon layer upon layer of abstraction, I picture the situation as our world held up by the four elePHPants, and then it's turtles all the way down.

It's time to take on one more component of the computer science ecosystem—the compiler. I think of diving into compiler internals as moving "down the stack." Is it safe? Of course it is! We'll see those friendly turtles all the way down.

Show Me the Code

PHP is open source, which means anyone can take a look. However, it's not as easy as with the various PHP frameworks, because PHP is written in C and makes heavy use of C preprocessor macros. We'll see it's relatively readable once we know how and where to look.

One value of open source software (OSS) is that we can take a look at any portion and see how it works. Depending on the project's license, we can freely modify, fix, enhance, and document to meet our current project's need. That's particularly easy when the library or framework is written in the same language.

For example, I do various PHP projects using the CakePHP framework[4]. It's written in PHP, and I can view the complete source code on GitHub[5]. I can report problems, suggest solutions, provide fixes; that's the beauty of open source software.

When the project is written in a different programming language contributing is more difficult. The PHP compiler/interpreter is written in C, with a small portion in C++. It also uses Lex (a parser-generating language), Yacc (a compiler-generating language), a

---

[3]   *So you want to work in security?*: https://phpa.me/want-work-security
[4]   *CakePHP framework*: https://cakephp.org
[5]   *GitHub*: https://github.com/cakephp

configurator (awareness of the target computer's hardware and operating system capabilities), and runs our PHP program on a virtual machine. That's a lot to take in.

Is there value in learning how PHP works internally? Certainly!

- First and foremost, much of the World Wide Web runs on PHP. We all, directly or indirectly, depend on it; contributions to PHP itself help all of us.

- The more we each know how PHP works "under the covers," the more effectively we can use PHP as we implement large projects that use PHP as the language of choice.

Learn by Doing

There's a way any of us can begin contributing immediately. It's greatly needed. Go to https://bugs.php.net and look at bug triage. You already know how to do this!

- Can you understand the problem as described?

- Can you reproduce (verify) the problem?

- Can you narrow down the problem to a specific environment, version, or context?

- Can you create a minimal test case which shows the problem?

- Can you add to the problem description to help clarify what the underlying issue is, or is not?

Anything you can do to make it easier for a core team member to read the bug report and fix (or otherwise resolve) the problem is a good thing. You've contributed to the forward progress of PHP itself!

One striking characteristic of PHP is the community. In contributing to bug triage—something every PHP programmer can do—you're taking a step in getting to know the PHP Internals community. Relationship-building takes time; begin to build that trust by being helpful!

Learn by Studying

I learn from books. If you're interested in learning more about compilers in general, here are two books I've found useful.

- *Implementing Programming Languages: An Introduction to Compilers and Interpreters*[6] has the advantage of being compact—under 200 pages. Many projects benefit from developing mini-languages (a domain-specific language). The book's examples

---

[6] *Implementing Programming Languages: An Introduction to Compilers and Interpreters:* https://www.amazon.com/dp/1848900643

alternate between Java and Haskell. For me, this book was an excellent refresher on the terminology (and symbols) used in language parsers and interpreters.

- The "Dragon Book" **Compilers: Principles, Techniques, and Tools, 2nd Edition**[7], so-called because of the dragon on the cover of the first edition. After more than a decade it remains ridiculously expensive, $180, but the "international economy edition" can be had from Amazon for $25. The economy edition seems to have lost a few dozen pages from this thousand-page monster, but I can live with that. I studied compilers long before the Dragon Book first appeared in 1986 (Figure 7.3), so I'm now reading the Second Edition (2006) right alongside you.

The Dragon Book is the gold standard for understanding how computer programs work. It's thorough and quite readable—in small doses.

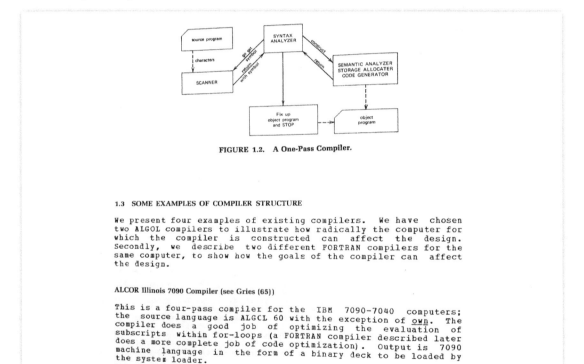

FIGURE 1.2. A One-Pass Compiler.

1.3 SOME EXAMPLES OF COMPILER STRUCTURE

We present four examples of existing compilers. We have chosen two ALGOL compilers to illustrate how radically the computer for which the compiler is constructed can affect the design. Secondly, we describe two different FORTRAN compilers for the same computer, to show how the goals of the compiler can affect the design.

ALCOR Illinois 7090 Compiler (see Gries (65))

This is a four-pass compiler for the IBM 7090-7040 computers; the source language is ALGCL 60 with the exception of own. The compiler does a good job of optimizing the evaluation of subscripts within for-loops (a FORTRAN compiler described later does a more complete job of code optimization). Output is 7090 machine language in the form of a binary deck to be loaded by the system loader.

Figure 7.3. Compiler Construction For Digital Computers (1971)

[7] *Compilers: Principles, Techniques, and Tools, 2nd Edition:*
https://www.amazon.com/dp/0321486811

The *PHP Internals Book*[8], a work in progress, includes a list of recommendations for learning how to program in C[9].

The official PHP site includes the out-of-date *PHP at the Core: A Hacker's Guide*[10]. The preface says it's current as of PHP 5.3.3. That's old. The information there *might* be useful as a general guide when you're trying to understand a specific topic.

The Blogs

One of the best ways to learn how PHP works is by looking at the code. Let's dive in and do just that. C syntax is close enough to PHP syntax that reading won't be too difficult.

To help you understand what the code is doing, here are three critical online resources:

- Blog by nikic[11] by Nikita Popov—essays on specific internals topics. He's placed similarly informative explanations on Stack Overflow. If you're researching a question and come across an answer by "nikic" you can be confident the answer is authoritative. You may find video presentations on YouTube as well.

- Ircmaxell's Blog[12] by Anthony Ferrara—parts are an extension of Popov's blog and are linked from there.

- The *PHP Internals Book* (linked previously), by Julien Pauli, Nikita Popov, Anthony Ferrara—a work in progress with chapters for both PHP 5 and PHP 7.

As our starting point, we'll be taking advantage of Ferrara's and Popov's series *PHP's Source Code for PHP Developers*[13]. They wrote this in 2012, but we'll be looking at a more recent (PHP 7.3) codebase. Let's dive right in.

Ferrara explains:

> As a PHP developer, I find myself referencing PHP's source code more and more in my regular everyday work. It's been instrumental in everything from understanding what's happening behind the scenes to figuring out weird edge cases to see why something that should be working isn't. Moreover, it's also handy in the cases when the documentation is either missing, incomplete, or wrong. So, I've decided to share what

---

[8]   PHP Internals Book: http://www.phpinternalsbook.com
[9]   program in C: https://phpa.me/php7-internals-intro
[10] PHP at the Core: A Hacker's Guide: http://php.net/internals2
[11] Blog by nikic: https://nikic.github.io
[12] Ircmaxell's Blog: https://blog.ircmaxell.com
[13] PHP's Source Code for PHP Developers: https://phpa.me/phps-src-devs

> *I've learned in a series of posts designed to give PHP developers enough knowledge to read the C source code behind PHP. No prior knowledge of C should be necessary (we'll cover some of the basics), but it helps.*

PHP Source

We can browse the PHP source at https://github.com/php/php-src. It's a mirror of the official repository at https://git.php.net, but if you peek at the official repository, you'll see it's far more difficult to browse; we'll stay with the GitHub mirror.

Scroll down the mirror page to the README.md information. (GitHub, by convention, always displays the top-level README file's contents on the front page of any repository.) Here the internals mailing list is named along with guidelines for contributing.

At this point, there's no real need for downloading (cloning) your copy of PHP source, or for attempting to build PHP for development. That PHP build can be a challenge for a different day!

Browsing Source

Up until around 2014, the PHP community maintained an excellent online tool at lxr.php.net[14]. It's no longer there, but as Ferrara explains:

> *This basically is an auto-generated searchable listing of source code, that's also syntax highlighted and fully linked. This is what I use almost exclusively for browsing the C source code; it's that good. Even when I'm making patches, I still reference lxr instead of the codebase I'm working on.*

Fortunately, Adam Harvey[15] provides a copy online with the following disclaimer[16]:

> *It's flaky because OpenGrok is flaky, so I haven't really gone out of my way to advertise it. We use it at $dayJob, though, so it should be up most of the time. Enjoy!*

The instructions and screenshots for this chapter were written using Harvey's courtesy copy. There will hopefully be an official version back in service by the time you read this. Please use the official version if one is currently available.

---

[14] lxr.php.net: http://lxr.php.net
[15] Adam Harvey: https://twitter.com/LGnome
[16] disclaimer: https://phpa.me/lgnome-91584

Figure 7.4. Browser Top

Visit the PHP source browser[17]. Note you can double-click on any branch listed in the right-hand box to begin browsing the source tree (Figure 7.4).

You've already noticed, by browsing the to the GitHub repository, there's a lot to take in. We have a dozen top-level directories and several dozen top-level files. We'll focus on two top-level directories:

- Zend is the Zend Engine, which contains the compiler/interpreter itself, including the language features and virtual machine.

- ext contains the extensions that constitute PHP's core.

All of the core functions such as strpos, substr, array_diff are in the extensions directory but the Zend Engine also contains some of these. The PHP Manual[18] top-level page provides a general guide. There's a section titled "Language Reference" and a section "Function Reference." Things found in "Language Reference" are generally in the Zend directory, and "Function Reference" things are in ext.

The list near the top of Zend/zend_builtin_functions.c includes func_num_args, func_get_arg, strlen, strcmp, etc.

This is why lxr is so useful. It's easiest to search for what you need—but you'll need to know a trick or two to find what you seek. Let's find some code.

---

[17] *PHP source browser: https://php-lxr.adamharvey.name/source/*
[18] *PHP Manual: http://php.net/manual/*

String Position

The following code walk-through is based on Popov's Understanding PHP's internal function definitions[19].

The strpos function finds "the position of the first occurrence of a substring in a string." You may be already familiar with PHP's string functions, but now is the time to re-check the manual page[20] and note some details:

- strpos was present in PHP 4, 5, 7.
- strpos has two required parameters and a third optional parameter.
- The method signature[21] says it returns an int but it also returns FALSE (if the needle was not found).
- $needle should be a string but it's allowed to be an int. When an int rather than string, the number is interpreted as the ASCII value of a one-character string. This behavior is weird, and deprecated as of PHP 7.3.
- $offset can be a negative number as of PHP 7.1.
- The function is binary-safe[22].

Let's walk through the code. Searching lxr for strpos yields 98 results as shown in Figure 7.5. That's useless.

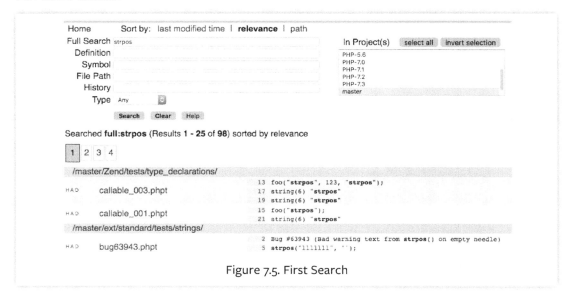

Figure 7.5. First Search

---

[19] Understanding PHP's internal function definitions: https://phpa.me/nikic-function-defs

[20] manual page: http://php.net/function.strpos

[21] method signature: https://en.wikipedia.org/wiki/Type_signature

[22] binary-safe: https://en.wikipedia.org/wiki/Binary-safe

Instead, search "`PHP_FUNCTION strpos`" including the double quotes. That's what we need—the public declaration and the function implementation. Both are in the `ext/standard` directory of the `master` branch (see Figure 7.6).

Let's look at the first result, line 44 of `php_string.h`. We see many lines that look similar to each other. In fact, they look rather pointless as captured in Figure 7.7.

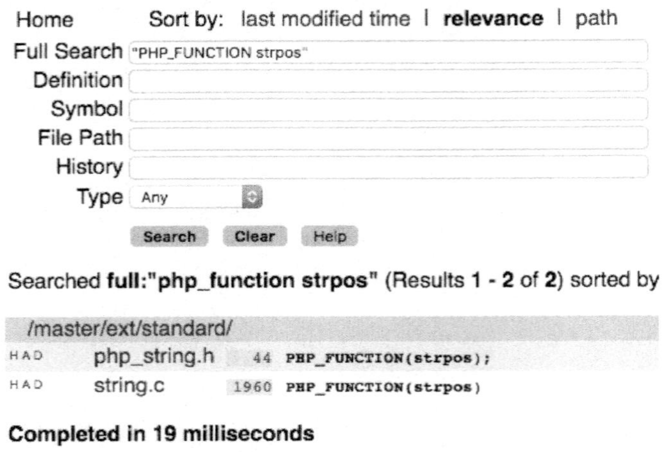

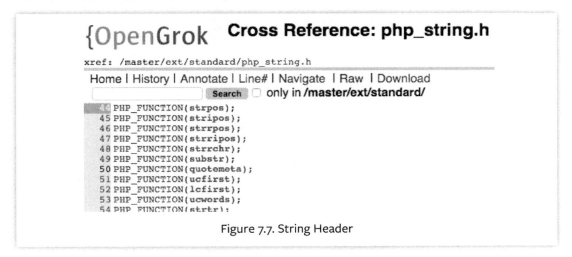

Figure 7.6. Search with Quotes

Figure 7.7. String Header

In C programming an .h file is called a "header" file. In this case, it's serving a similar purpose to a PHP Interface file. C header files include the public declaration of constants, data structures, and function names.

In C, you must declare all functions before calling them from somewhere else. C projects, like PHP projects, can potentially have many thousands of files, and we don't know in what order they'll be evaluated. C uses header files to provide the list of things that need to be known.

In PHP we have use, include, require, and autoloaders to ensure an outside class can be invoked or referenced when needed. In C we don't load the entire class file. We only load the relevant header file declaring that the function (or data structure or constant) exists.

Now that we know this, we can skip right past the header-file declaration and move on to the source file string.c. The corresponding file is also on GitHub at ext/standard/string.c[23].

Click on the search result https://phpa.me/php-lxr-string-1960 and back up two lines to include the user manual documentation.

Now we're hitting C code head-on (Figure 7.8). Let's do our best to interpret what each line of code means.

Lines 1958-1959 contain the same information as the function signature in the PHP manual. I'm guessing the one is likely generated from the other.

```
/* {{{ proto int strpos(string haystack, string needle [, int offset])
   Finds position of first occurrence of a string within another */
```

```
1957
1958 /* {{{ proto int strpos(string haystack, string needle [, int offset])
1959    Finds position of first occurrence of a string within another */
1960 PHP_FUNCTION(strpos)
1961 {
1962    zval *needle;
1963    zend_string *haystack;
1964    const char *found = NULL;
1965    char  needle_char[2];
1966    zend_long  offset = 0;
1967
1968    ZEND_PARSE_PARAMETERS_START(2, 3)
1969            Z_PARAM_STR(haystack)
1970            Z_PARAM_ZVAL(needle)
1971            Z_PARAM_OPTIONAL
1972            Z_PARAM_LONG(offset)
1973    ZEND_PARSE_PARAMETERS_END();
1974
```

Figure 7.8. Search Result

[23] ext/standard/string.c: https://phpa.me/php-src-stringc

As for the {{{ `proto` part, I notice line 2015 at the end of the function:

```
/* }}} */
```

Those look like markers for the beginning and end of the function, with the beginning saying we're declaring the function prototype.

Next is line 1960:

```
PHP_FUNCTION(strpos)
```

Everything we've seen so far tells us we're now looking at the code implementing PHP's standard `strpos()` function. The trouble is that `PHP_FUNCTION` isn't part of the C programming language. A standard C function looks like this:

```
int foo()
{
  return 0;
}
```

However, C also has something called the preprocessor, cpp. The preprocessor supports macros. C preprocessor macros are simple text substitution but are extremely powerful because they support input parameters. For example:

```
#define TIMESTWO(a) ((a) * 2)
int b = TIMESTWO(3);
```

gets rendered as:

```
int b = ((3) * 2);
```

You'll have noticed two things:

- C variables do not begin with $. Instead of $a and $b like PHP, we simply write a and b.
- The above macro appears to have way too many parentheses. `((3) * 2);` could as well have been written as `3 * 2;`.

However, the C preprocessor is doing text substitution, not variable interpolation or anything of the sort. Suppose instead we had:

```
#define WIDTH 60
#define WRONG(a) (a * 2)
#define TIMESTWO(a) ((a) * 2)
int b = WRONG(WIDTH + 12);
int c = TIMESTWO(WIDTH + 12);
```

After preprocessing, the latter two lines become:

```
int b = (60 + 12 * 2);
int c = ((60 + 12) * 2);
```

Do you see the difference? We're doing pure text substitution here. What's passed in could be a complicated expression produced from macros calling macros calling macros. (It's like turtles all the way down!) That's why we'll see every parameter usage contained inside parentheses. The final result is contained inside parentheses so, when it, in turn, gets passed into some other macro, the order of expression evaluation remains the same.

Since we're curious to see what PHP_FUNCTION actually does, let's guess it's a macro definition and search "define PHP_FUNCTION". There's only one result, main/php.h line 400. Lines 396-401 are:

```
/* PHP-named Zend macro wrappers */
#define PHP_FN          ZEND_FN
#define PHP_MN          ZEND_MN
#define PHP_NAMED_FUNCTION    ZEND_NAMED_FUNCTION
#define PHP_FUNCTION      ZEND_FUNCTION
#define PHP_METHOD        ZEND_METHOD
```

And so it goes. We're chasing from one macro to another. (It really is turtles all the way down!) Let's search "define ZEND_FUNCTION". That takes us to Zend/zend_API.h line 64. We need lines 61-65:

```
#define ZEND_FN(name) zif_##name
#define ZEND_MN(name) zim_##name
#define ZEND_NAMED_FUNCTION(name)      void ZEND_FASTCALL name(INTERNAL_FUNCTION_PARAMETERS)
#define ZEND_FUNCTION(name)          ZEND_NAMED_FUNCTION(ZEND_FN(name))
#define ZEND_METHOD(classname, name)  ZEND_NAMED_FUNCTION(ZEND_MN(classname##_##name))
```

Let's back up and remember where we were. We were looking at the strpos() function declaration in ext/standard/string.c. We decided to "jump down the rabbit hole" and see if we could see what the declaration PHP_FUNCTION(strpos) really means. We found that PHP_FUNCTION is an alias for ZEND_FUNCTION.

Now it gets tricky! Let's do the text substitutions based on the above preprocessor macros.

1. PHP_FUNCTION(strpos) *becomes:*
2. ZEND_FUNCTION(strpos) *becomes:*
3. ZEND_NAMED_FUNCTION(ZEND_FN(strpos)) *becomes:*
4. ZEND_NAMED_FUNCTION(zif_##strpos))

```
245 #if defined(__GNUC__) && ZEND_GCC_VERSION >= 3004 && defined(__i386__)
246 # define ZEND_FASTCALL __attribute__((fastcall))
247 #elif defined(_MSC_VER) && defined(_M_IX86) && _MSC_VER == 1700
248 # define ZEND_FASTCALL __fastcall
249 #elif defined(_MSC_VER) && _MSC_VER >= 1800 && !defined(__clang__)
250 # define ZEND_FASTCALL __vectorcall
251 #else
252 # define ZEND_FASTCALL
253 #endif
254
```

Figure 7.9. Fast Call

The ## operator—yes it is an operator, not a delimiter—is the C preprocessor's token concatenation operator[24]. It works much like PHP string interpolation in "string{$variable}ify".

In the above example, the input parameter is strpos, so after the substitution, we have zif_strpos. I believe "zif" stands for "Zend internal function." We'll see why that's significant in a moment. To continue with our text substitutions:

1. ZEND_NAMED_FUNCTION(zif_strpos) *becomes:*
2. void ZEND_FASTCALL zif_strpos(INTERNAL_FUNCTION_PARAMETERS)

We'll stop there. However, a search for "define ZEND_FASTCALL" does show how C preprocessor conditionals work.

Notice the sequence of #if, #elif, #else, #endif in Figure 7.9. It works just as you would expect. The defined() preprocessor function works as it does with PHP; the symbol is defined at that point, or it isn't. Line 247 checks to see if _MSC_VER is defined and equal to 1700.

I know when using the GNU C compiler gcc, it defines the symbol[25] __GNUC__. I'm guessing, on Windows, the Microsoft C compiler defines the symbol _MSC_VER and the symbol's value is the compiler's version. Thus, we are defining ZEND_FASTCALL a bit differently depending on which compiler processes our source code.

The Microsoft documentation repository on GitHub explains __fastcall[26] is a Microsoft-specific "calling convention." It "specifies that arguments to functions are to be passed in registers, where possible."

Where does this get us? We noticed references to "zif" meaning (I believe, but might be wrong here) "Zend internal function," the function signature containing "internal function

---

[24] *token concatenation operator:* https://phpa.me/cpp-concatenation
[25] *defines the symbol:* https://phpa.me/gcc-common-macros
[26] *__fastcall:* https://phpa.me/ms-cpp-fastcall

parameters" and references to "fast call" meaning a particular optimized way of calling the strpos() function.

What this all probably means is that the core functions are called more efficiently than standard userland functions. That makes sense! After compiling the PHP source code, our function is probably called zif_strpos, but we know in the source code it is PHP_FUNCTION(strpos).

We have now examined two lines of comments (lines 1958-59) and one line of executable code (line 1960). Let's pick up the pace!

Lines 1962-66 shown in Figure 7.10 declare local variables for strpos: needle, haystack, found, needle_char, offset. They are not declared in the same order as the parameter list—that doesn't matter. We'll get back to those variables in a moment.

Lines 1968-73 copy the runtime input parameters to the local variables. When we call strpos from our code, we pass in the search string and target (haystack, needle, optional offset). Lines 1968-73—all preprocessor macros—take care of copying those values to the local variables declared lines 1962-66.

In the PHP compiler/interpreter, all user variables are called a "zval" meaning "Zend engine value." A zval can be any PHP type. A zend_string is a particular type of zval—a PHP string.

Line 1968 is the start of the parameter-copying sequence; line 1973 is the end. Note that only line 1973 finishes with a semicolon; these likely become one single C statement.

1. (2, 3) indicates we have two required parameters and three total.
2. The first parameter is a string and copied to local variable haystack.
3. The second parameter could be anything and is copied to needle.

```
1957
1958 /* {{{ proto int strpos(string haystack, string needle [, int offset])
1959    Finds position of first occurrence of a string within another */
1960 PHP_FUNCTION(strpos)
1961 {
1962    zval *needle;
1963    zend_string *haystack;
1964    const char *found = NULL;
1965    char  needle_char[2];
1966    zend_long  offset = 0;
1967
1968    ZEND_PARSE_PARAMETERS_START(2, 3)
1969            Z_PARAM_STR(haystack)
1970            Z_PARAM_ZVAL(needle)
1971            Z_PARAM_OPTIONAL
1972            Z_PARAM_LONG(offset)
1973    ZEND_PARSE_PARAMETERS_END();
1974
```

Figure 7.10. Declare Local Variables

4. The third parameter, if present, is an integer and copied to offset. A PHP integer becomes a "long" in C, and PHP float becomes "double" in C.

What if we want to learn the gory details of how parameter passing works? Use the lxr search just like we did to drill down through PHP_FUNCTION.

Lines 1975-1981 check the offset:

```
if (offset < 0) {
    offset += (zend_long)ZSTR_LEN(haystack);
}
if (offset < 0 || (size_t)offset > ZSTR_LEN(haystack)) {
    php_error_docref(NULL, E_WARNING, "Offset not contained in string");
    RETURN_FALSE;
}
```

Line 1966 initialized offset to 0. If we passed the optional parameter, it was copied into offset. If it's negative, it's defined as counting from the end of the string, so add it to the string length. If it's out of range, issue a PHP warning error. If the error was suppressed (did not cause an exception), return false.

We can probably read the "happy path" well enough:

```
1.    if (Z_TYPE_P(needle) == IS_STRING) {
2.        if (!Z_STRLEN_P(needle)) {
3.            php_error_docref(NULL, E_WARNING, "Empty needle");
4.            RETURN_FALSE;
5.        }
6.
7.        found = (char*)php_memnstr(ZSTR_VAL(haystack) + offset,
8.                        Z_STRVAL_P(needle),
9.                        Z_STRLEN_P(needle),
10.                       ZSTR_VAL(haystack) + ZSTR_LEN(haystack));
```

If the needle is a string (rather than an integer, which would be weird), check to see if we're searching for an empty string. Trying to find an empty string makes no sense, so issue a warning error and return FALSE.

Otherwise, we're on the happy path. Call php_memnstr() with the search and target strings, lengths, offsets. A quick lxr search tells us php_memnstr is really zend_memnstr at line 148 in Zend/zend_operators.h.

Wait a moment! That's weird. We have a full function declaration (lines 147-187) in a header file, not a .c file. Why is that? It's intended to be "always inline." That means it's not a separate function; it is compiled in-place every time, for efficiency's sake. This optimization makes sense; we do many string searches in our PHP code!

The above code is used when the needle is a string. Here is the "else" part, i.e., when the needle is an integer.

```
1.    } else {
2.        if (php_needle_char(needle, needle_char) != SUCCESS) {
3.            RETURN_FALSE;
4.        }
5.        needle_char[1] = 0;
6.
7.        php_error_docref(NULL, E_DEPRECATED,
8.            "Non-string needles will be interpreted as strings in the future. " \
9.            "Use an explicit chr() call to preserve the current behavior");
10.
11.       found = (char*)php_memnstr(ZSTR_VAL(haystack) + offset,
12.                   needle_char,
13.                   1,
14.                       ZSTR_VAL(haystack) + ZSTR_LEN(haystack));
15.   }
```

In C, strings are character (byte) arrays. The final character is a zero byte. A one-character string, therefore, is an array of two bytes. The first byte is the character and the second byte is a zero.

Here we attempt to convert the integer needle to a one-byte character, which we place into needle_char[0]. We set needle_char[1] to a zero, thus creating a zero-terminated string of length one. We then throw the E_DEPRECATED error and search the string.

Our function ends:

```
if (found) {
    RETURN_LONG(found - ZSTR_VAL(haystack));
} else {
    RETURN_FALSE;
}
}
```

If we found the needle in the haystack, by whatever means, we return the offset at which we found the needle. Otherwise we return false.

We could verify our reading of the code and the PHP manual page with some test code. I'm interested in seeing if I can hit that "deprecated" message, but I can't reproduce it. Why?

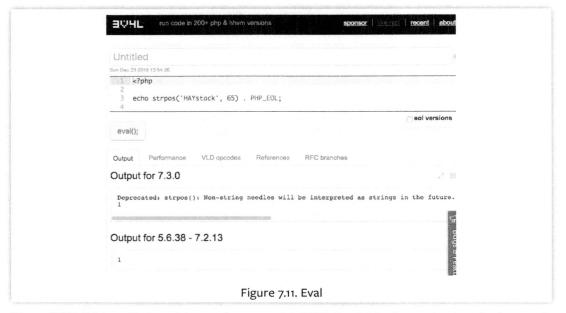

Figure 7.11. Eval

I have PHP 7.2 installed, and it was deprecated at PHP 7.3. We've been viewing the "master" branch in the GitHub repository which includes PHP 7.3.

There's an online tool at https://3v4l.org (that's "leet speak" for "eval") which evaluates PHP code using different PHP versions. Let's try it out. Output is shown in Figure 7.11.

The uppercase A is ASCII 65, which is offset 1 for HAYstack. PHP 7.3 issues the deprecated warning message with the result 1. PHP versions 5.6 through 7.2 issue just the result, integer 1.

To be sure, we glossed over various things we need to know with C programming, particularly how C pointers (the * operator) work. Even so, we could pretty well see how the function works, even without C programming.

Summary

We've now walked through strpos. We learned various tools and techniques for navigating and exercising the PHP compiler code (written in C) such as lxr. We have links to books and blogs. I particularly recommend Nikita Popov's blogs as a great starting point for additional reading. We have a recommended starting point for helping the PHP core developers: bug triage.

Chapter
8

Deep Dive

We're taking a deep dive into the PHP compiler (written in C). We're going to focus on how PHP implements arrays. However, understanding C code requires far more than understanding the language syntax. We need to understand the environment and context. This means we'll need to continue learning how computers and software work.

This chapter is our most intense from a software-development standpoint. We'll be applying a lot of the knowledge we've been gaining, but in a modern (2019) context. If you find yourself winded in this chapter, skip forward to the next chapter, _Impostor Syndrome_. You'll have clear sailing from there on out. Here, in this chapter, there be dragons.

Aristotle[1], in *On the Heavens* (c. 350 BC), ridiculed the idea that the Earth is stationary simply because it is spherical and any forces on it must be equal in all directions. He explained that the idea is as ridiculous as saying that:

> *A man, being just as hungry as thirsty, and placed between food and drink, must necessarily remain where he is and starve to death.*

I have a similar quandary when setting out to explore or become familiar with a large codebase that's new to me. When everything seems just as important, or just as unimportant, it's hard to know where to start. I pick one aspect, feature, or topic to use as my focus.

That's the situation with the PHP compiler/interpreter. It's a large and unfamiliar codebase. I, therefore, picked one specific topic—how PHP implements arrays at runtime as something called a hash table.

We'll start by looking at runtime PHP. We'll then proceed to PHP's "packed" hash table implementation, then see how regular (non packed) hash tables work. Finally, we'll learn some C coding idioms needed to understand the PHP compiler/interpreter source code.

PHP and C

PHP is a C-like language. Assuming you know PHP it's not hard—in theory—to read C code. The syntax is quite similar. Variables, control structures, loops, all look roughly the same between the two languages. You'd recognize an `if`/`else` block or `for` loop and know what it does. When you see a `do ... while()` you would correctly guess the flow of control works exactly like in PHP.

PHP's runtime system, written in C, can be hard to follow. The C code embraces unfamiliar patterns and ways of doing things. Unfamiliar, that is, to us as PHP developers partly because preprocessor macros hide so much. It's not the C syntax that's the difficulty; it's how the code was written that's the difficulty. It'll make sense once we understand those patterns and their context, but we're not there yet.

Let's address that difficulty head-on. We're going to take a deep dive into one aspect of PHP, namely how arrays are implemented. The implementation itself is the easy part; Wikipedia fully describes the theory. The challenge is in the side issues.

We'll learn to identify common programming patterns in the C code. These are patterns not encountered in PHP code and thus are likely to be unfamiliar.

---

[1]   Aristotle: https://en.wikipedia.org/wiki/Buridan%27s_ass

The PHP runtime system is "close to the hardware." That is, the C code assumes you're entirely comfortable with two's complement arithmetic; shifting and masking; Boolean operations; and so on. We'll need to be constantly aware of the actual binary representation of a variable as it magically shifts between signed and unsigned usage.

That's why our "deep dive" needs to cover a lot of territory. We need to understand how computers and computer programs work, at a fundamental level, to understand the PHP runtime context. We won't be digging through the code quite yet.

Let's begin by looking at what it is that runs.

File Execution

C code gets compiled down to "object code," file by file. The object files (.o files) get collected together and transformed into a single executable file in ELF[2] format. That's true for Unix/Linux systems. The process is similar on Windows systems, producing a .exe file, but I don't know any of the details.

The executable file was historically called "the binary" because it contains the runnable machine instructions comprising your computer program(s). It's not a text file—you can't simply open up the binary file and make much sense of it. Machine instructions are "binary." A copy of the runnable program ("the executable" or "the binary") was often placed in the bin directory (with "bin" standing for "binary") so it could be found.

We still follow this convention on modern Unix/Linux systems. PHP's composer, for example, places a copy of phpunit and other tools in the vendor/bin directory in your source tree when installing locally.

In this sense, Shell scripts, Perl scripts, PHP scripts, and binary ELF files are all considered executable and can go in the bin directory. Unix/Linux also requires the file to have appropriate execute permission, or the operating system won't allow direct invocation (run).

How do we distinguish between an ELF file, which can be loaded and run directly, a Shell script, a Perl script, or a PHP script? For scripting languages, the filename extension (such as .pl for Perl and .php for PHP) tells you and me that the operating system should pass the file to the relevant language interpreter. That operating system, however, needs more information.

We can read the first few bytes as the file's magic number[3]. Shell scripts begin with #! followed by the path to the program that should run the file (such as /bin/sh). This marker

---

[2]   ELF: *https://phpa.me/wikip-elf-format*
[3]   *magic number:* *https://phpa.me/wikip-magic-number*

is called the shebang line[4]. The "she" comes from the hash character #, and the exclamation point ! is generally pronounced "bang" by C and Unix/Linux operating system programmers.

For example:

```
#!/bin/bash
echo Here we go...
```

An ELF file's magic number, the first four bytes of the file, is 0x7f followed by ASCII ELF. Java bytecode (that is, compiled Java class files) uses the magic number 0xCafeBabe ("cafe babe"). Compressed Java bytecode uses magic number 0xCafeD00d ("cafe dude"). Two hexadecimal digits make up one byte; the four-byte magic number requires eight hexadecimal digits.

Use the file command on Unix/Linux to interpret the file's magic number. For example, file /bin/bash yields:

```
$ file /bin/bash
/bin/bash: Mach-O 64-bit executable x86_64
```

To see the first few bytes of the file, dump it out with od -h ("octal dump" as hexadecimal).

```
od -h /bin/bash | head -1
0000000   facf   feed   0007   0100   0003   8000   0002   0000
```

If we search online for 0xfacffeed, nothing turns up. That's because my MacBook Pro laptop with this copy of /bin/bash is little-endian[5]. The first chunk and second chunk are swapped. The actual magic number is 0xFeedFacf, that is, "feed face" plus one. The list of known hexadecimal-number jokes is online as hexspeak[6].

Let's look at mach-o/loader.h[7] which defines this magic number. See Listing 8.1.

Listing 8.1. Mach-o/loader.h

```
1. /*
2.  * The mach header appears at the very beginning of the object file; it
3.  * is the same for both 32-bit and 64-bit architectures.
4.  */
5. struct mach_header {
```

---

[4]   shebang line: https://phpa.me/wikip-shebank
[5]   little-endian: https://en.wikipedia.org/wiki/Endianness
[6]   hexspeak: https://en.wikipedia.org/wiki/Hexspeak
[7]   mach-o/loader.h: https://phpa.me/xnu-mach-loader

```
 6.      uint32_t    magic;      /* mach magic number identifier */
 7.      cpu_type_t cputype;     /* cpu specifier */
 8.      cpu_subtype_t  cpusubtype; /* machine specifier */
 9.      uint32_t    filetype;   /* type of file */
10.      uint32_t    ncmds;      /* number of load commands */
11.      uint32_t    sizeofcmds; /* the size of all the load commands */
12.      uint32_t    flags;      /* flags */
13. };
14.
15. /*
16.  * The 64-bit mach header appears at the very beginning of object files for
17.  * 64-bit architectures.
18.  */
19. struct mach_header_64 {
20.      uint32_t    magic;      /* mach magic number identifier */
21.      cpu_type_t cputype;     /* cpu specifier */
22.      cpu_subtype_t  cpusubtype; /* machine specifier */
23.      uint32_t    filetype;   /* type of file */
24.      uint32_t    ncmds;      /* number of load commands */
25.      uint32_t    sizeofcmds; /* the size of all the load commands */
26.      uint32_t    flags;      /* flags */
27.      uint32_t    reserved;   /* reserved */
28. };
29.
30. /* Constant for the magic field of the mach_header (32-bit architectures) */
31. #define MH_MAGIC    0xfeedface  /* the mach magic number */
32. #define MH_CIGAM    NXSwapInt(MH_MAGIC)
33.
34. /* Constant for the magic field of the mach_header_64 (64-bit architectures) */
35. #define MH_MAGIC_64 0xfeedfacf  /* the 64-bit mach magic number */
36. #define MH_CIGAM_64 NXSwapInt(MH_MAGIC_64)
```

Now it all fits together. Apple uses "feed face" for mach_header and "feed facf" for mach_header_64. This is why the file command reports /bin/bash as a "Mach-O 64-bit executable x86_64" based on the magic number and following bytes in the above-described structure. The above C header file is fairly readable. We can make guesses and get a general idea.

Note that CIGAM is MAGIC spelled backward. The symbol MH_MAGIC is "feed face," and MH_CIGAM is the same value with the bytes swapped. The prefix MH_ no doubt refers to the structure definition "mach header."

This bit of weirdness deals with the fact that the executable could have been created (compiled) on big-endian hardware with the target system (where it runs) being little-endian, or vice versa. This process, where the compiling system and target system are not the same, is called *cross compiling*.

Cross-compiling is quite frequent (and necessary). A widespread distribution, such as the PHP compiler/interpreter, needs to be built for many different target architectures. The same build process, running on the same system, is often responsible for producing the many different target versions (often called "build artifacts") for distribution.

For example, the PHP For Windows[8] download page includes eight variants for each of the currently-supported releases. The variants include builds for x64 and x86 architecture; thread-safe and non-thread-safe for each architecture; and a debug pack for each of these builds.

Cross-compiling is also typical for embedded systems. A host system is responsible for building the software to be loaded onto the embedded (target) system.

How is this excursion into "feed face" even relevant to running PHP? It's relevant because we're getting to know the runtime environment. We can't just focus on the source code. We must understand its environment and context, or nothing makes sense.

Now we'll know what we see when we extract the same information from PHP itself. We use which php to produce the full path of the file in question.

```
$ od -h `which php` | head -1
0000000   facf   feed   0007   0100   0003   8000   0002   0000

$ file `which php`
/usr/bin/php/php7.2.1/bin/php: Mach-O 64-bit executable x86_64
```

However, if we examine the file binary, we find an Apple "universal binary," also called the "fat" file format (not to be confused with the FAT file format) because it contains multiple binaries inside the same file:

---

[8] PHP For Windows: *https://windows.php.net/download*

```
$ file `which file`
/usr/bin/file: Mach-O universal binary with 2 architectures: [x86_64:Mach-O
64-bit executable x86_64] [i386:Mach-O executable i386]
/usr/bin/file (for architecture x86_64): Mach-O 64-bit executable x86_64
/usr/bin/file (for architecture i386):   Mach-O executable i386

$ od -h `which file` | head -1
0000000    feca  beba  0000  0200  0001  0700  0080  0300
```

The file program, here, says we have two executable versions—one for 64-bit x86 architecture, and one for i386 architecture.

The magic number is 0xfecabeba. Except that it isn't. The bytes are swapped. "fe ca" gets swapped to become "ca fe." "be ba" also needs to be swapped, to become "ba be." This magic number is "cafe babe," the Java magic number.

We've now seen "big-endian" and "little-endian" byte swapping. In the first case, a 16-bit chunk was swapped with the next 16-bit chunk. In the last case, each 8-bit chunk was swapped with the next 8 bits. We have two different byte-swapping procedures in executable files on the same hardware.

In my view, this illustrates the general difficulty we're trying to overcome. Things won't make sense until you figure out their context. The context often turns out to derive from some weirdness that happened back in the 1990s or even 1950s.

Java[9], for example, was named after the coffee. That makes sense given the close cultural ties between caffeine and software development. The magic number[10] identifying Java bytecode class files was "originally created by NeXTSTEP developers as a reference to the baristas at Peet's Coffee & Tea." NeXTSTEP[11], based on Unix, was developed by NeXT Computer, which was later bought by Apple, and became macOS and iOS.

That's why, to this day, "Cafe Babe" identifies Apple Universal Binaries. The sexism remains baked into our Silicon Valley software.

Wikipedia's *Comparison of executable file formats*[12] explains Linux and most versions of Unix use ELF, and macOS and iOS use Mach-O. Wikipedia has a separate article on Apple's *Universal Binary*[13] format.

---

[9]   Java: *https://phpa.me/wikip-java*
[10] magic number: *https://en.wikipedia.org/wiki/Hexspeak*
[11] NeXTSTEP: *https://en.wikipedia.org/wiki/NeXTSTEP*
[12] Comparison of executable file formats: *https://phpa.me/wikip-compare-exec*
[13] Universal Binary: *https://phpa.me/wikip-universal-bin*

We've now looked at one aspect of runtime PHP, namely, examining the files that run—the binaries.

Let's move on to PHP itself.

Runtime PHP

PHP source code, like Java source code, gets compiled down to bytecode and run on a virtual machine. The Java object code is persisted as a JAR[14] (Java Archive) file. PHP has no equivalent.

The terms *bytecode*, *oplines*, and *opcodes* are more or less equivalent when discussing PHP internals. The *opcode*, specifically, refers to which instruction is being used, e.g., "add" versus "multiply." The full executable statement, which is the opcode with operands, is the *opline*. Our compiled PHP program could be called either bytecode or oplines—or just called the opcodes.

PHP's OPcache[15] "improves PHP performance by storing precompiled script bytecode in shared memory, thereby removing the need for PHP to load and parse scripts on each request."

Our PHP program, as bytecode, is executed by the PHP 7 Virtual Machine[16]. Thus we have a program executing a program.

The PHP virtual machine is written in C. The PHP script `Zend/zend_vm_gen.php`[17] generates the C code. Thus we have a C program, generated by a PHP program, that is executing your PHP program, as bytecode coming from OPcache.

PHP's virtual machine gives us platform independence, the same as does the Java Virtual Machine (JVM). The same bytecode could, in theory, execute on any platform. We just saw Java does this. Those are the JAR files.

PHP compiles and caches our source code but makes no provision for distributing that compiled code between platforms.

The other reason PHP requires a virtual machine is its complex set of rules and edge cases. Nikita Popov's article *PHP 7 Virtual Machine* describes, as an example, the gruesome process of exception handling. Where the exception was thrown is one context; unwinding the call stack to find the `catch` block places us in another context; executing `finally` imposes yet another context.

---

[14] JAR: *https://phpa.me/wikip-java-jar*
[15] OPcache: *http://php.net/intro.opcache*
[16] PHP 7 Virtual Machine: *https://phpa.me/nikic-php7-vm*
[17] `Zend/zend_vm_gen.php`: *https://phpa.me/php-src-zend-vm-gen*

In addition to PHP's virtual machine, which is executing your PHP program (as byte-code), we have the rest of PHP. PHP comes with built-in string functions such as `strpos`, built-in array functions such as `array_fill`, and so on. PHP stores your variables in a format called a `zval` and structures your arrays in a hash table[18]. We'll learn about the hash table below.

Once your PHP code is running on the virtual machine, it's primarily the Zend Engine Zend[19] and the PHP Extensions ext[20] that are running. We can see the PHP language implementation, in C, in the `Zend` directory, and the PHP functions in the `ext` directory.

It's not always clear whether a given function can be found in `Zend` or `ext`. Anything in the PHP manual's Function Reference[21] is likely in `ext` and anything in the Language Reference[22] is likely in `Zend`. However, "built-in" functions such as `property_exists` are in `Zend` even though they're described in the Function Reference. It's a large codebase; you'll need to search for what you need.

Hash Table

Let's look at PHP's array implementation. PHP implements arrays as a hash table[23]. Figure 8.1 showing a small phone book as a hash table comes from the Wikipedia article.

The *hash table* is a data structure designed for handling key-value pairs. PHP arrays are ordered maps of keys to values. The hash table is designed for rapid mapping of keys to values, that is, given the key quickly find the value.

In a typical C array, for example, to find element five, you'd skip down the array to element five. However, with PHP the array key can also be a string.

We don't want to do a sequential search for that array key. As the array grows larger and larger, the access time would get worse and worse. We want the access time to be fast, *very* fast, no matter how large the array gets.

The hash table algorithm provides that speed. How does it work?

The hash table uses a *hash function* to compute an *index* into an array of *buckets* or *slots*. The hash function attempts to spread our array values evenly across the available buckets.

---

[18] hash table: https://phpa.me/wikip-hash-table
[19] Zend: https://phpa.me/php-src-zend
[20] ext: https://phpa.me/php-src-ext
[21] Function Reference: http://php.net/funcref
[22] Language Reference: http://php.net/langref
[23] hash table: https://en.wikipedia.org/wiki/Hash_table

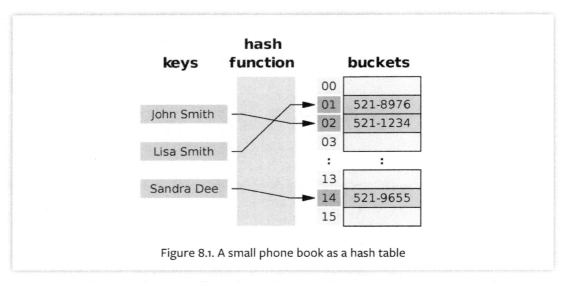

Figure 8.1. A small phone book as a hash table

An imperfect hash function allows for collisions. When two array keys map to the same bucket slot, that's called a collision. We'll explore how PHP hash maps handle collisions later.

Perfect Hash Function

When all keys are known ahead of time, we can create a *perfect hash function* which provides us a hash table with no collisions.

A common PHP use case is the ordered list such as [1, 1, 2, 3, 5, 8] where the array keys begin with zero and increase by one. With $a = [1, 1, 2, 3, 5, 8], we have six array elements $a[0] through $a[5]. PHP recognizes this as the special case (where the array keys are consecutive integers beginning with zero) and stores it using a perfect hash function.

The perfect hash function is far more efficient than any *imperfect hash function*. An imperfect hash function, as we'll see later, needs to follow collision chains. Here, with the perfect hash function, the array key is the slot index.

In this example, PHP allocates eight buckets (a power of two) numbered 0 through 7. The array key 0 through 5 is the bucket number. To look up $a[5], PHP extracts the value from bucket number 5. The PHP code (written in C) calls this particular case a *packed hash table*.

Packed Hash Table

Given the PHP code:

```
$a = [1, 1, 2, 3, 5, 8];
```

Our hash table looks like Figure 8.2.

The array key is the same as the bucket slot. A PHP integer has zval type IS_LONG.

We iterate through the array by iterating through the bucket slots, from 0 to the end. The hash table keeps track of the table size as follows:

- The total table size (eight in this case) is nTableSize.

- The number of buckets in use (six in this case), and therefore, the next available bucket slot, is nNumUsed.

- The number of valid elements (also six in this case) is nNumOfElements.

If we append a value like this:

```
$a[] = 'Feed';
```

Our hash table now looks like Figure 8.3.

At this point nTableSize remains eight (the total number of buckets allocated); nNumUsed is now seven; nNumOfElements is also seven. The value type IS_STRING means what you expect; the value is a PHP string. The zval data types are in Zend/zend_types.h[24] around line 382.

Packed Hash Table

Bucket Slot	Type	Value
0	IS_LONG	1
1	IS_LONG	1
2	IS_LONG	2
3	IS_LONG	3
4	IS_LONG	5
5	IS_LONG	8
6	Not initialized	
7	Not initialized	

Figure 8.2. Packed Hash Table

Packed Hash Table

Bucket Slot	Type	Value
0	IS_LONG	1
1	IS_LONG	1
2	IS_LONG	2
3	IS_LONG	3
4	IS_LONG	5
5	IS_LONG	8
6	IS_STRING	Feed
7	Not initialized	

Figure 8.3. Packed Hash Table

In a packed hash table, when there is room, we can add more array elements to the end of the array. The unused buckets after the end of the array remain uninitialized because they might never be needed.

However, when we do need them (by appending elements to the array, with incrementing keys), we initialize them "just in time," that is, as they are about to be used. This happens in Zend/zend_hash.c[25] function _zend_hash_index_add_or_update_i (currently line 957), but we're not ready to dig into the source code just yet.

---

[24] Zend/zend_types.h: https://phpa.me/php-src-zend-types
[25] Zend/zend_hash.c: https://phpa.me/php-src-zend-hash

We can also unset array elements, leaving the rest of the array intact. For example:

```
unset($a[0], $a[4]);
```

Unsetting two array elements leaves our packed hash table looking like Figure 8.4.

Now nNumOfElements is five. This would be the value returned by PHP count($a). The next available slot nNumUsed remains seven. The table size nTableSize remains eight.

We can still iterate through the array as before. We merely ignore (skip over)

Packed Hash Table

Bucket Slot	Type	Value
0	IS_UNDEF	
1	IS_LONG	1
2	IS_LONG	2
3	IS_LONG	3
4	IS_UNDEF	
5	IS_LONG	8
6	IS_STRING	Feed
7	Not initialized	

Figure 8.4. Packed Hash Table

any bucket whose value type is IS_UNDEF. We stop iterating once we've examined nNumUsed buckets.

The PHP Language Reference on arrays[26] explains "an array in PHP is an ordered map." Packed hash tables often need to be converted to regular hash tables.

When PHP code creates an array without specifying the keys, we'll use the more-efficient packed array. Where we're adding to the array without specifying a key (as in our example above), we can still use a packed array.

As soon as we begin specifying our array keys, the above scheme will no longer work. It's limited to integer keys incrementing from zero. Also, because PHP arrays are an ordered map, if we unset a key and then use it again:

```
unset($a[0], $a[4]);
$a[0] = 'Face';
```

We can no longer store the array in "packed" format. That's because array elements remain in the order they were added to the array. When we iterate through the updated array, 0 => 'Face' comes at the end.

The packed hash table can increase in size. Let's create an array and add several elements.

```
$b = [1, 1, 2, 3, 5, 8, 13];
$b[] = 21;
$b[] = 34;
$b[] = 55;
```

---

[26] arrays: http://php.net/language.types.array

Our array can still be stored in a packed hash table, but it's doubled in size to contain 16 buckets.

1. When first creating the array with seven elements, we allocated a large enough slab of memory to contain eight buckets. We initialized the first seven buckets, placing the seven values in those buckets. nTableSize is eight, nNumUsed is seven, nNumOfElements is seven.

2. When appending value 21, we initialized the eighth bucket (bucket seven), set the value type to IS_LONG, and the value to 21.

3. When appending value 34, we discovered we're out of room. We allocate a new slab of memory large enough to contain 16 buckets. We copy the old slab of memory's contents (i.e., the buckets) over to the new slab of memory. The buckets are each a continuous slab of memory, so this is a fast and efficient operation. We then release (deallocate) the old slab of memory. nTableSize is 16, nNumUsed is 9, nNumOfElements is nine.

4. Append 55 as above. Now nTableSize remains 16, nNumUsed is 10, nNumOfElements is 10. Bucket slots 10-15 remain uninitialized.

Why would we build packed hash tables if we might need to convert them to regular hash tables later? Isn't there a lot of overhead involved in the conversion?

Yes, and no. The numeric array is such a typical case that it's far more efficient to keep it as a packed hash table. Think about your PHP code; when an array starts with numeric keys, how often does it get out of order? How often do we add string keys to a numerically-indexed array? Chances are good it can remain as a packed hash table throughout the life of that array.

When we do need to convert the packed hash table to a regular hash table, screaming-fast C code converts it. That conversion happens only once, if at all, for any given PHP array.

It's time to learn about regular, non-packed, hash tables. We'll have collisions.

Hash Table Collisions

As we continue our deep dive into how PHP implements arrays as hash tables, it's time to see how the collision chain works. We're not ready to dig into the C implementation just yet, so we'll see how to build and rebuild the hash table using PHP code. Here we're learning how PHP arrays are stored and manipulated; later, we'll see the C code itself.

Thus far we've seen how PHP treats simple arrays as a special case. Where the array keys are all numeric, starting at zero and incrementing by one, we can store the array using a *perfect hash function.* The array elements are stored in *buckets* and the array key becomes the bucket number.

A perfect hash function is one where no collisions are possible. PHP does not allow duplicate array keys, so the mapping of array key to bucket number works perfectly for numerically indexed arrays (so long as other conditions are met as we've seen).

However, PHP also allows strings as array keys with no limit on string length or content. We can mix string keys and integer keys in the same array. If a string key is numeric and does not start with +, it is converted to an integer key. PHP even converts float keys to integer keys and null to the empty string as a key.

I've never seen anyone use a floating-point number as a PHP array key. Don't do it! However, since the language supports this sort of key transformation, the PHP engine (written in C) needs to allow for edge cases like this.

When the array key is a string, PHP uses a hashing function to produce the numeric hash h. When the key is already an integer, PHP uses that integer key as the numeric hash h. We then reduce the hash h down to an index idx that fits within the range of the current hash table.

PHP arrays can be any size, ranging from an empty array up to arrays containing millions of elements or more. A separate hash table sized accordingly contains each array. Thus, the index idx for a small hash table has a much smaller range than the index idx for a large hash table.

The hash table must, therefore, compute both the hash h and the index idx separately. The hash h remains the same for a given key and is, therefore, stored in the bucket along with the array element. But the index idx can change as the size of the hash table changes.

Array Key	Hash	idx	value
0	0	-1	"red"
foo	-2	-2	"blue"
bar	-72	-4	"green"
4	4	-5	"purple"

For example, if the hash table has room for eight buckets (array elements), the index idx is limited to eight possible values. However, if the hash table has room for 1,048,576 elements, the idx can be anywhere in that range.

Of course, for a given hash table size, the mapping of hash h to index idx is always the same. We need to be able to always find the same array element in the same bucket, every time! (Buckets can get moved, but that's a separate discussion.)

Collision Resolution

Wikipedia explains how PHP handles hash table[27] collisions.

> *Hash collisions are practically unavoidable when hashing a random subset of a large set of possible keys. For example, when hashing 2,450 keys into a million buckets, even with a perfectly uniform random distribution, according to the birthday paradox[28] there is an approximately 95 percent chance of hashing at least two of the keys to the same slot.*

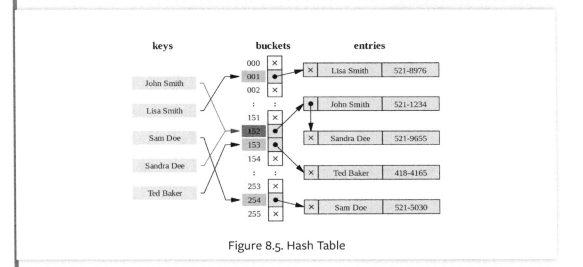

Figure 8.5. Hash Table

> *Therefore, almost all hash table implementations have some collision resolution strategy to handle such events. These methods require storing the keys (or pointers to them) in the table, together with the associated values.*

PHP uses *separate chaining* for collision resolution (Figure 8.5), which Wikipedia explains:

[27] *hash table: https://en.wikipedia.org/wiki/Hash_table*
[28] *birthday paradox: https://phpa.me/wikip-birthday-problem*

> *Each bucket is independent and has some list of entries with the same index. The time for hash table operations is the time to find the bucket (which is constant) plus the time for the list operation.*
>
> *In a good hash table, each bucket has zero or one entries, and sometimes two or three, but rarely more than that. Therefore, structures that are efficient in time and space for these cases are preferred. Structures that are efficient for a relatively large number of entries per bucket are not needed or desirable. If these cases happen often, we need to fix the hashing function.*

Dynamic Resizing

As we saw previously, PHP hash tables grow by powers of two. When the table size is a power of two, the index calculation is more efficient. The index calculation is a bitwise OR (|), as we'll see in Listing 8.3. The alternative would be a modulus calculation (%), which is generally slower on modern computer hardware.

When a hash table of size 64, for example, needs more capacity, the interpreter resizes it to 128. More precisely, when the current hash table is size nTableSize, and n more elements are needed, the new size should be nTableSize + n rounded up to the next power of two.

If the current table size is 128, and 1,000 more elements are needed, the new table size is 2,048 (the next higher power of two). If the current table size is eight, and eight more elements are needed, the new table size is 16.

PHP never shrinks a hash table. It only expands the hash table. To expand the hash table, we allocate a new slab of memory large enough to hold the entire new hash table. We then copy the old hash table to the new slab of memory. (We'll explain what that slab of memory is, and how big it is, in a future article. We'll need to know quite a few incidental things first.)

Both the old hash table and the new hash table are contiguous chunks of memory. Therefore, copying the old table's content to the new table is extremely rapid and efficient.

PHP is designed for web applications. The life of a PHP program is the duration of a single webpage load. Array allocations tend to be short-lived. Doubling the array size, as needed, provides a reasonable balance between using as little memory as possible and avoiding the overhead of too many expansions.

The PHP memory limit comes into play here. Large arrays play into that limit. I've had to increase memory limits when importing large spreadsheets (500,000-line CSV files), for example.

Let's look at some examples. *Be warned! The rest of this chapter is heavy going as we see precisely how PHP (written in C) handles arrays as hash tables. There be dragons.*

PHP Hash Table

First, we make an array which uses strings for keys.

```
$a = [
    'the' => 'article',
    'book' => 'noun',
    'read' => 'verb'
];
```

This creates a hash table of size 8 (the minimum size). For each element, we calculate the hash h using a hashing function and map that to a table index value idx. (I'm using a different hashing function for this example.) Figure 8.6 shows the hashing results.

Hashing Results (table size 8)

Key	Key Type	Hash	Index	Value Type	Value
the	string	-37359206	-6	IS_STRING	article
book	string	-1098126045	-5	IS_STRING	noun
read	string	-2679714455	-7	IS_STRING	verb

Figure 8.6. Hash Table

With a table size eight, our hash table contains eight hash slots and eight bucket slots. The table looks like Figure 8.7.

PHP (written in C) constructs the table as follows. The negative offsets (-8 through -1) are the hash slots (explained below). The non-negative offsets (0 through 7) are the bucket slots.

1. We need room for three elements. The minimum table size is eight. Set nTableSize to 8. Set nTableMask, used in computing the index idx, to -8.

2. Initialize the table, setting the hash index values to -1 (an out-of-range number). Set the number of elements

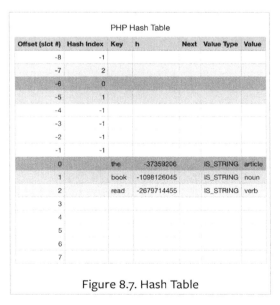

PHP Hash Table

Offset (slot #)	Hash Index	Key	h	Next	Value Type	Value
-8	-1					
-7	2					
-6	0					
-5	1					
-4	-1					
-3	-1					
-2	-1					
-1	-1					
0		the	-37359206		IS_STRING	article
1		book	-1098126045		IS_STRING	noun
2		read	-2679714455		IS_STRING	verb
3						
4						
5						
6						
7						

Figure 8.7. Hash Table

used, nNumOfElements, to 0. Set the next available bucket number nNumUsed to 0.

3. Place the first element 'the' => 'article' in the first available bucket, bucket 0. Store the hash value -37359206 as h. Store the value type as IS_STRING. Since the key is a string, store the key in the bucket as key. key is null when the array key is an integer. The integer key used as the hash value and stored in h. Increment nNumUsed and nNumOfElements.

4. We computed the hash index as -6. We, therefore, store the bucket number, which is 0, at slot -6. The two pink rows are now filled in, in the figure.

5. Follow the same process for 'book' => 'noun'. This is the pair of blue rows. The next available bucket is bucket 1. The computed index is -5, so store the bucket number 1 in slot -5. Increment nNumUsed and nNumOfElements.

6. The third element, 'read' => 'verb' is the pair of yellow rows. It takes the next bucket, bucket 2. The key 'read' maps to hash index -7. The hash slot at -7 now contains the bucket number, 2.

Now unset the first element:

```
unset($a['the']);
```

PHP Hash Table

Offset (slot #)	Hash Index	Key	h	Next	Value Type	Value
-8	-1					
-7	2					
-6	-1					
-5	1					
-4	-1					
-3	-1					
-2	-1					
-1	-1					
0					IS_UNDEF	
1		book	-1098126045		IS_STRING	noun
2		read	-2679714455		IS_STRING	verb
3						
4						
5						
6						
7						

Figure 8.8. Hash Table with Holes

Hashing Results (table size 8)

Key	Key Type	Hash	Index	Value Type	Value
the	string	-37359206	-6	IS_STRING	article
book	string	-1098126045	-5	IS_STRING	noun
read	string	-2679714455	-7	IS_STRING	verb
hash	string	-4129918790	-6	IS_STRING	table
bucket	string	-2886606951	-7	IS_STRING	slot
string	string	-2324736937	-1	IS_STRING	key
throw	string	-1347160907	-3	IS_STRING	fit
expand	string	-4129918790	-6	IS_STRING	table
size	string	-3672634095	-7	IS_STRING	double
PHP	string	-2212294583	-7	IS_LONG	1
C	string	-450215437	-5	IS_LONG	2

Figure 8.9. Hash Calculations

The pink row gets marked as undefined. nNumOfElements (the count of active elements, count($a)) is decremented but nNumUsed (the next available bucket slot) remains the same. When nNumOfElements < nNumUsed, we have one or more holes in the table (see Figure 8.8).

Let's add more array elements. We'll see collisions. We'll need to compact the table. We'll later expand the table. First, do the hash calculations (Figure 8.9).

Add 'hash' => 'table'. The result is in green in Figure 8.10. New elements go into the next bucket slot, nNumUsed++. The hash index is -6, so slot -6 now contains the bucket number, 3.

Offset (slot #)	Hash Index	Key	h	Next	Value Type	Value
-8	-1					
-7	2					
-6	3					
-5	1					
-4	-1					
-3	-1					
-2	-1					
-1	-1					
0					IS_UNDEF	
1		book	-1098126045		IS_STRING	noun
2		read	-2679714455		IS_STRING	verb
3		hash	-4129918790		IS_STRING	table
4						
5						
6						
7						

Figure 8.10. New Element

When we next add 'bucket' => 'slot', we have a collision. Both string keys read and bucket map to hash index -7. Here's what we do.

1. Place the array element in the next available bucket, nNumUsed++, which is bucket 4.

2. Our hash index is -7. Copy that value, 2, to the next field in our bucket, bucket 4.

3. Update the hash slot to contain our current bucket number. In other words, update the hash slot -7, which did contain a 2, to contain 4.

Our hash table now looks like Figure 8.11. Our new element is in orange.

Notice that our array has remained ordered. We can correctly iterate through the array by iterating through bucket slots 0 through 4 and skipping any elements with

Offset (slot #)	Hash Index	Key	h	Next	Value Type	Value
-8	-1					
-7	4					
-6	3					
-5	1					
-4	-1					
-3	-1					
-2	-1					
-1	-1					
0					IS_UNDEF	
1		book	-1098126045		IS_STRING	noun
2		read	-2679714455		IS_STRING	verb
3		hash	-4129918790		IS_STRING	table
4		bucket	-2886606951	2	IS_STRING	slot
5						
6						
7						

Figure 8.11. New Element

PHP Hash Table

Offset (slot #)	Hash Index	Key	h	Next	Value Type	Value
-8	-1					
-7	4					
-6	7					
-5	1					
-4	-1					
-3	6					
-2	-1					
-1	5					
0					IS_UNDEF	
1		book	-1098126045		IS_STRING	noun
2		read	-2679714455		IS_STRING	verb
3		hash	-4129918790		IS_STRING	table
4		bucket	-2886606951	2	IS_STRING	slot
5		string	-2324736937		IS_STRING	key
6		throw	-1347160907		IS_STRING	fit
7		expand	-4129918790	3	IS_STRING	table

Figure 8.12. Full with Hole

IS_UNDEF values. The next available bucket slot is nNumUsed, which is currently five. nNumOfElements is the array count, four. The table size, nTableSize, is eight.

Let's add three more elements.

1. Key string, with hash index -1, has no collisions. It goes in bucket 5.
2. Key throw, with hash index -3, has no collisions. It goes in bucket 6.
3. Key expand, with hash index -6, is a collision. It goes in bucket 7 with next set to 3 (the next bucket in the collision chain).

Our hash table is now full, though it has a hole in it. Bucket 0 is unused, as shown in Figure 8.12.

How do we retrieve an array value? For example:

```
$choice = $a['read'];
```

1. We take the string key read and compute the hash value.
2. From that, we compute the hash index, -7.
3. Hash slot -7 contains the bucket number, 4.
4. Bucket 4 contains the key bucket, confusingly enough which is *not* the key we seek. We seek the key read. Therefore we're dealing with a hash collision and need to walk the collision chain (the next field).

5. We check bucket 4's next field. It contains a bucket number, 2. We'll go to bucket 2 next.

6. Bucket 2 contains the key read. This *is* the key we seek.

7. We retrieve the array element value, verb, and copy it into the PHP variable $choice. The hash table remains unchanged.

Compact Hash Table

If we need to add another element to the hash table, we have a problem. We're out of space. However, if the hash table has enough holes (unused buckets), PHP compacts the table in place. This "bubbles up" the unused buckets to the end of the table.

I'm not sure if one hole is enough to justify compacting. Let's look at the C code for making the decision in zend_hash_do_resize around line 1122 of Zend/zend_hash.c[29]:

```
if (ht->nNumUsed > ht->nNumOfElements + (ht->nNumOfElements >> 5)) {
    zend_hash_rehash(ht);
```

The above code includes the explanation "additional term is there to amortize the cost of compaction." With nNumUsed equal 8 and nNumOfElements equal 7, the additional term is (7 >> 5) which is 0, so we would call zend_hash_rehash to compact our hash table.

How did we figure out (7 >> 5) is zero? The C and PHP syntax are the same. It's a right shift by five bits. Seven, in binary, is 0000 0111. A right shift of one bit (for example) would produce 0000 0011. That is, the rightmost bit gets shifted off the end, and a zero gets brought in from the left. If the leftmost bit were a one, additional ones would be brought in from the left. Since the leftmost bit is called the sign bit, we call this sign-bit propagation. For more, read about PHP's bitwise operators[30].

Therefore, when we right-shift 0000 0111 five bits, the result is all zeroes, 0000 0000, which is zero. Our if calculation becomes:

```
if (8 > 7 + 0)
```

C, as with PHP, does the addition before it makes the comparison. The if test evaluates to true, and we call zend_hash_rehash.

The actual C code for zend_hash_rehash (around line 1141 of Zend/zend_hash.c) is rather wild. We have a lot to cover before we're ready for that particular chunk of code. Instead, I wrote a PHP implementation of the same function. The variable and function names match the C implementation.

---

[29] Zend/zend_hash.c: https://phpa.me/php-src-zend-hash
[30] bitwise operators: http://php.net/language.operators.bitwise

You can download the PHP code from ewbarnard/InsidePHP[31] on GitHub. The hash table implementation is at InsidePHP/inside_php/src/ZendEngine3[32]. We'll be looking at ZendEngine3/Hash/HashRehash.php. See Listing 8.2.

Listing 8.2. HashRehash01.php

```php
1.  <?php
2.  class HashRehash01 {
3.      public static function zend_hash_rehash(HashTable $ht): int {
4.          if (HashRehash::isEmptyArray($ht)) {
5.              return HashRehash::clearEmptyArray($ht);
6.          }
7.
8.          if (HashTable::HT_IS_PACKED($ht)) {
9.              return HashRehash::clearPackedArray($ht);
10.         }
11.
12.         if (HashTable::HT_HAS_ITERATORS($ht)) {
13.             // Zend/zend_hash.c line 1186
14.             // @codeCoverageIgnoreStart
15.             throw new \Exception('Not supporting hash table with iterators');
16.         }
17.         // @codeCoverageIgnoreEnd
18.         HashTable::HT_HASH_RESET($ht);
19.
20.         if (HashTable::HT_IS_WITHOUT_HOLES($ht)) {
21.             return HashRehash::rehashNoHoles($ht);
22.         }
23.
24.         return HashRehash::rehashHoles($ht);
25.     }
26. }
```

Here's the top-level flow. Ours is not an empty array; it's not a packed hash table (covered earlier). It does not have internal iterators, so we skip past the first three if checks.

At line 18, HT_HASH_RESET, we clear all the hash slots to -1 (the invalid bucket number). We skip past the next if check, because our hash table *does* have holes.

Next, we'll walk through HashRehash::rehashHoles. See Listing 8.3.

---

[31] ewbarnard/InsidePHP: *https://github.com/ewbarnard/InsidePHP*
[32] InsidePHP/inside_php/src/ZendEngine3: *https://phpa.me/inside-php-zend3*

Listing 8.3. HashRehash02.php

```php
 1. <?php
 2. class HashRehash02 {
 3.     public static function rehashHoles(HashTable $ht): int {
 4.         $currentBucketSlot = 0;
 5.         $unusedBucketSlot = -1;
 6.         do {
 7.             if (HashRehash::bucketSlotUnused($ht, $currentBucketSlot)) {
 8.                 $ht->arData[$currentBucketSlot] = null;
 9.                 if ($unusedBucketSlot < 0) {
10.                     $unusedBucketSlot = $currentBucketSlot;
11.                 }
12.             } else {
13.                 if ($unusedBucketSlot >= 0) {
14.                     // Bring the bucket down to the unused slot, effectively
15.                     // bubbling-up the unused slot to the next position
16.                     $ht->arData[$unusedBucketSlot] = $ht->arData[$currentBucketSlot];
17.                     $ht->arData[$currentBucketSlot] = null;
18.                     $currentBucketSlot = $unusedBucketSlot;
19.                     $unusedBucketSlot = -1;
20.                     $ht->arData[$currentBucketSlot]->bucketSlot = $currentBucketSlot;
21.                 }
22.             }
23.         } while (++$currentBucketSlot < $ht->nNumUsed);
24.         $ht->nNumUsed = $ht->nNumOfElements;
25.         return HashRehash::rehashNoHoles($ht);
26.     }
27. }
```

Since, in my implementation, our bucket slots merely contain pointers to Bucket objects, we don't need to copy buckets from one slot to the other. We can shift the pointer from the old slot to the new slot.

The do ... while walks through the bucket slots. If we find a slot that's unused (i.e., the bucket value type is IS_UNDEF) we remember that slot as $unusedBucketSlot.

Otherwise, the bucket slot is being used. Move the in-use bucket down to the unused slot. We continue walking from that unused-now-used slot.

Our unused bucket has now bubbled-up to the end of the table, bucket 7. nNumUsed and nNumOfElements are both seven, and the table size nTableSize remains eight.

Notice how we used the loop variable, $currentBucketSlot. We increment it at the bottom of the do ... while, but we also reset it to a smaller value any time we move a bucket down to an unused bucket slot. In effect, we are taking "two steps forward, one step back."

This technique is relatively common in the underlying C code when walking through a slab of memory or a collection of things. It's perfectly legal in C to modify the loop variable in the midst of the loop. Just make sure the looping does eventually finish!

Next, we repopulate the hash slots. See Listing 8.4.

Listing 8.4. HashRehash03.php

```php
1.  <?php
2.  class HashRehash03 {
3.      public static function rehashNoHoles(HashTable $ht): int {
4.          $bucketSlot = 0;
5.          do {
6.              HashRehash::rehashBucketSlot($ht, $bucketSlot);
7.          } while (++$bucketSlot < $ht->nNumUsed);
8.          return ZendTypes::SUCCESS;
9.      }
10.
11.     public static function rehashBucketSlot(HashTable $ht, int $bucketSlot): void {
12.         /** @var Bucket $bucket */
13.         $bucket = $ht->arData[$bucketSlot];
14.
15.         $hashSlot = $bucket->h | $ht->nTableMask;
16.         $bucket->val->u2_next = $ht->arData[$hashSlot];
17.         $ht->arData[$hashSlot] = $bucketSlot;
18.     }
19. }
```

These few lines of code rebuild the now-compacted hash table. To understand it, though, we need the context. There's a bit more to explain the collision chain.

The bucket next pointer (the collision chain) always points to a lower-numbered bucket slot or is a negative number (meaning invalid, i.e., we have reached the end of the chain). When there are no collisions, the next pointer will, therefore, be a negative number (or possibly null in this PHP simulation).

Bucket slots are >= 0, and hash slots are < 0. The hash table contains *both* the hash slots and buckets in that single slab of memory (in the real C code).

The hash slot's value is the number of a bucket slot, or -1 to indicate it's an unused hash slot. Bucket slots contain a bucket pointer, or null to indicate it's an unused bucket slot (in this simulation).

The hash slot always points to the highest-numbered bucket slot of a collision chain. We start high and work our way low. The bucket's next pointer, if any, always points to a lower-numbered bucket slot. In the real C implementation next is a pointer—here it is merely a slot number.

When there are no gaps in the bucket slots, we can rehash the hash table by walking through the bucket slots, from slot 0 up to the highest slot currently in use.

1. For the bucket slot, compute the corresponding hash slot.
2. Take the hash slot's current value and store it in the bucket's next field.
3. Store the current bucket slot number as the new hash slot's value.

In this way, we rebuild the hash collision chain as we go. The hash slot keeps getting updated to the highest-numbered bucket using this hash value, and the bucket gets the next-lower slot in the collision chain.

The "collision chain" is the list of all PHP array keys that map to the same hash slot number. For example, in this implementation (using crc32 as the hashing function), both PHP numeric array key 1, or the value for string array key read map to hash slot -7, when the hash table is the minimum size of eight.

When looking up the value for array key 1, or the value for array key read, both lead us to hash slot -7. Each bucket stores both the PHP value we're seeking, and the actual PHP array key (either 1 or read in this case). We walk through the buckets until we find the bucket with our array key, or hit the end of the chain (key not found).

In the listing, rehashNoHoles walks through the buckets starting at zero. We call rehashBucketSlot to rehash that bucket.

rehashBucketSlot computes the hash slot index at line 15. It is a bitwise OR of the computed array key's hash, OR-d with the hash table mask (which is -8 in this case). How does that work?

In two's complement integer representation, which is what is happening here, the value -1 is all ones in binary. The largest (most-negative) negative number, in binary, contains the sign bit (the left-most bit) followed by all zeroes.

In two's complement notation, when the sign bit is set, the number is negative. Always. When the sign bit is set, and the remaining bits are all ones, that's -1, which is the least-negative number. When the sign bit is set, and the rest of the bits are all zeroes, that's the most-negative number.

Do you see the pattern? So long as the sign bit is set, the more bits you set to one, the closer the number gets to -1. -8, in binary, is 11111 ... 11111000. So, listing line 15:

```
$hashSlot = $bucket->h | $ht->nTableMask;
```

Ensures that $hashSlot is a value that's at least -8 and at most -1. That's our hash index calculation.

Line 16 sets the current bucket next value to the previous value that was in the hash slot. The value might be -1, indicating we're at the end of the collision chain.

Line 17 sets the hash slot value to our current bucket number.

Now, finally, we're ready to look at the C code itself. We'll learn some of the programming patterns to be seen in the C code so that we can more quickly recognize what a given piece of code is doing.

Patterns in the Code

The PHP compiler source code includes many patterns that can be frustrating and intimidating, because they are so different from typical PHP code, until we understand the structure and context. C's preprocessor has a significant role in these unfamiliar patterns. Let's look at several of these patterns in the compiler's PHP Array implementation.

Working With the Codebase

Where shall we start? With a large codebase, that's always a problem. We're focused on the array implementation, called hash tables in the source code. The three files of interest are:

- Zend/zend_types.h[33]—the different types of variables, but also hash table details.
- Zend/zend_hash.h[34]—here is the API information for using hash tables, but a whole lot more; we need to talk.
- Zend/zend_hash.c[35]—the array (hash table) implementation; it's opaque until you get used to it.

---

[33] Zend/zend_types.h: https://phpa.me/php-src-zend-types
[34] Zend/zend_hash.h: https://phpa.me/php-src-zend-hash-hdr
[35] Zend/zend_hash.c: https://phpa.me/php-src-zend-hash

Don't forget the cross-reference tool lxr[36] we used in *Turtles All The Way Down*. It is your friend.

Function Declaration

The source code is difficult to follow until you get used to it. Let's take a few lines (Zend/zend_hash.c near line 1056) to illustrate the problem. See Listing 8.5.

Listing 8.5. Zend Hash Set Bucket Key

```
1. ZEND_API zval* ZEND_FASTCALL zend_hash_set_bucket_key(HashTable *ht,
   Bucket *b, zend_string *key)
2. {
3.     uint32_t nIndex;
4.     uint32_t idx, i;
5.     Bucket *p, *arData;
6.
7.     IS_CONSISTENT(ht);
8.     HT_ASSERT_RC1(ht);
9.     ZEND_ASSERT(!(HT_FLAGS(ht) & HASH_FLAG_PACKED));
10.
11.    p = zend_hash_find_bucket(ht, key, 0);
12.    if (UNEXPECTED(p)) {
13.        return (p == b) ? &p->val : NULL;
14.    }
15.
16.    if (!ZSTR_IS_INTERNED(key)) {
17.        zend_string_addref(key);
18.        HT_FLAGS(ht) &= ~HASH_FLAG_STATIC_KEYS;
19.    }
```

We looked at function signatures earlier, so we can make educated guesses about line 1:

- ZEND_API implies this function signature is part of the internal API, i.e., that it's a public function callable from anywhere. (I guessed incorrectly; see below.)

- This function returns a pointer to a zval structure. Conceptually that's like how a PHP function/method can return a PHP object, which is a pointer to the object. (A zval is a general-purpose structure that can represent any type of PHP variable.)

- Tell the compiler to generate the "fast call" calling sequence if it can.

- The function requires three arguments—a HashTable structure pointer; a Bucket

---

[36] lxr: *https://php-lxr.adamharvey.name/source/*

structure pointer; a `zend_string` structure pointer.

When terms, such as "structure" or "calling sequence," aren't clear to me, I use Google. Most of the concepts are well described on Wikipedia, YouTube, or somewhere. We'll continue explaining below.

Let's use `lxr` to search `"define ZEND_API"` (with the quotes). We have six definitions, all similar. Let's check `Zend/configure.ac`[37]. The top line of the file says "Process this file with autoconf to produce a configure script."

The `ZEND_API` lines are:

```
#if defined(__GNUC__) && __GNUC__ >= 4
# define ZEND_API __attribute__ ((visibility("default")))
#else
# define ZEND_API
#endif
```

According to the GCC Wiki[38] "visibility" is a C++ feature that:

- Very substantially improves load times of your DSO (Dynamic Shared Object)
- Lets the optimizer produce better code
- Reduces the size of your DSO by five to 20 percent
- Lowers the chance of symbol collision

This explanation clearly has nothing to do with PHP's array implementation. In fact, `ZEND_API` doesn't appear to have anything to do with declaring an API at all! What it does is tell the C compiler how to best generate the object code.

This is the difficulty with a large codebase. You'll need to jump down quite a number of rabbit holes to see how things are structured. At first, you won't be able to discern what's important at the moment and what isn't. In many cases, you can guess from the context and move on. Go back and drill down to the definition as needed. As we learn how more and more pieces fit together, we get a clearer picture of the whole. Eventually, it starts to click and make sense.

Variable Declaration

Lines 3-4 declare three variables `nIndex`, `idx`, and `i`. PHP best practice opts for long descriptive variable names. C practice is often the opposite. These days, typing speed is not the determining factor in how many lines of code are produced per day. When C was first in

---

[37] Zend/configure.ac: https://phpa.me/zend-configure
[38] GCC Wiki: https://gcc.gnu.org/wiki/Visibility

use, typing speed was a limiting factor; often the programmer typed the code across a slow connection. Picture typing your code on a phone screen, in an underground garage where you lose the cell phone signal every few minutes (just before clicking "save"), and you'll get the idea. Or, more commonly, the code was typed on a keypunch with no such thing as a backspace key. Whatever the reason, the "short variable name" habit has carried forward.

The variables are type `uint32_t` which is the same as `UNSIGNED INT` in MySQL. It's a 32-bit number with no negative numbers (no minus sign). The leftmost bit, normally the sign bit, has no particular meaning.

PHP has no similar concept. Neither does C, by the way, even though you see it here. C programmers have vast control over the C compiler and have wide latitude in telling it what object code to generate. `uint32_t` is a typedef[39], that is, a definition of a data type. The C standard library and POSIX reserve the suffix _t.

Typedef

Line 5 declares two `Bucket` pointers. How do we know what a `Bucket` is? In PHP, we would look for the `Bucket` class definition. In C it is likely to be in a header file, and we'll use `lxr` to find it. Click on any of the results, and then click on the word `Bucket`, and the click takes you to the definition around line 229 of `Zend/zend_types.h`[40]. See Listing 8.6.

Listing 8.6. Struct Bucket

```
typedef struct _Bucket {
    zval             val;
    zend_ulong       h;     /* hash value (or numeric index)  */
    zend_string      *key;  /* string key or NULL for numerics */
} Bucket;
#define getBucket(b, n) ((Bucket *)((b) + ((n) * sizeof(Bucket))))
```

Line 5 tells us `Bucket` is a `typedef struct _Bucket`. This is a common idiom in C, and it's somewhat like declaring class properties in PHP.

The C keyword `typedef` means "create an alias." For example:

```
typedef long scoped;
```

We have just created a data type called `scoped`. It is not a variable; it is a data type. In PHP we have `string`, `int`, `float`, and so on. In C we similarly have `char`, `long`, `double`. Now, instead of declaring a variable of type `long`, we can declare it of type `scoped`. It's weird but

---

[39] typedef: https://en.wikipedia.org/wiki/Typedef
[40] Zend/zend_types.h: https://phpa.me/php-src-zend-types

is used continuously in C header files. It's aimed at making the C code more intuitive and readable.

The C keyword struct describes a "structured" data type. In this case, _Bucket contains three fields. If we, therefore, declare a variable of type Bucket, that means the variable contains those three fields. We could set the h field in the bucket like this:

```
Bucket b;
b.h = 0;
```

The notation is somewhat like how JavaScript accesses object properties.

Memory Pointer

PHP, in comparison to C, is a refined, cultured language. C, by design, has all the power of an assembly language coupled with all the flexibility of an assembly language.

The Unix operating system was initially implemented[41] in assembly language. Because assembly code is tied closely to the bare metal, when moving to new hardware architecture, we can not port assembly-language programs. They need to be rewritten for the new platform. Since it had to be rewritten anyway, authors Dennis Ritchie and Ken Thompson considered rewriting it in a language called "B," which was Thompson's simplified version of BCPL.

However, B was unable to take advantage of some of the new hardware's features. It didn't have the power of an assembly language. Thus, C was invented to have all the power of an assembly language. The name "C" was chosen simply as the next after B.

As a side note, BCPL was created as a language for writing compilers. The fact that the PHP compiler is written in one of its direct successors, C, is both elegant and exceedingly obscure trivia. BCPL is a dead language, but its influence is still felt with Unix, Linux, iOS, and the existence of all C-like languages.

Straight-up C programming, as opposed to C++, C#, or other more-modern variants, is dangerous. A common outcome is the program ending (crashing) with a "segfault." Arrays, for example, have no bounds checks (by design!), so it's easy to corrupt the program space by storing an array value outside the array. C programmers need to be careful about memory management, pointer calculations—basically everything that's in the program space.

---

[41] *initially implemented:* *https://phpa.me/wikip-c-language*

> *Val Kilmer, Iceman: "You're everyone's problem. That's because every time you go up in the air, you're unsafe. I don't like you because you're dangerous."*
>
> *Tom Cruise, Maverick: "That's right, Iceman. I am dangerous."*
>
> — *Top Gun (1986)*

If you're coming from PHP and beginning to read C, remember it's designed to work closely with the hardware. It's designed to *be* the computer, to *see* the computer. (See what we did there, with B and C?) C is designed to be the operating system (Unix/Linux) and the compiler. C is about bits and bytes and memory locations.

A C variable is just an alias for a memory location. If a `Bucket` structure is 128 bytes, an array of ten Buckets would be 1280 bytes. Walking through the array of buckets would mean skipping forward 128 bytes at a time.

There's no such concept in PHP. In PHP, if we had an array of ten Bucket objects, the array would contain ten pointers to the ten objects.

In contrast, in C, we can ask for a slab of memory. The memory allocator provides the starting address of that slab of memory. Meanwhile, we have a `Bucket` pointer. Just stick the memory slab's location in that bucket pointer:

```
Bucket *b;
b = (Bucket *)malloc(...);
```

To move to the second bucket, still inside that single slab of memory, we increment the pointer by the size of the `Bucket` (128 bytes):

```
Bucket *nextBucket = b;
nextBucket += sizeof(Bucket);
```

We can produce bucket *n* as follows:

```
#define getBucket(b, n) ((Bucket *)((b) + ((n) * sizeof(Bucket))))
```

`sizeof(Bucket)` provides us the number of bytes in a bucket. Multiply that by *n* and we have the byte address for bucket *n* (counting from zero). Add that to the base address of the memory slab, and we have the address of bucket *n*.

By defining this as a macro, the result becomes inline code wherever the macro is used. We don't incur the overhead of a function call. The compiler may be able to optimize the code further using the surrounding context. The source code contains many such macros.

In Listing 8.5 line 5, `arData` is our pointer to that slab of memory. `p` points to the individual bucket inside that slab of memory.

More Macros

The next line of Listing 8.5 is `IS_CONSISTENT(ht)`. The macro is defined in
`Zend/zend_hash.c`. Why would it be defined in the `.c` file and not the header file? That, in
effect, means it's private. That macro is not available outside the one file. This macro definition is a useful pattern to recognize, so let's take a look. See Listing 8.7.

Listing 8.7. Zend Is Consistent

```
 1. #if ZEND_DEBUG
 2.
 3. #define HT_OK                    0x00
 4. #define HT_IS_DESTROYING         0x01
 5. #define HT_DESTROYED             0x02
 6. #define HT_CLEANING              0x03
 7.
 8. static void _zend_is_inconsistent(const HashTable *ht, const char *file, int line)
 9. {
10.     if ((HT_FLAGS(ht) & HASH_FLAG_CONSISTENCY) == HT_OK) {
11.         return;
12.     }
13.     switch (HT_FLAGS(ht) & HASH_FLAG_CONSISTENCY) {
14.         case HT_IS_DESTROYING:
15.             zend_output_debug_string(1, "%s(%d) : ht=%p is being destroyed", file, line, ht);
16.             break;
17.         case HT_DESTROYED:
18.             zend_output_debug_string(1, "%s(%d) : ht=%p is already destroyed", file, line, ht);
19.             break;
20.         case HT_CLEANING:
21.             zend_output_debug_string(1, "%s(%d) : ht=%p is being cleaned", file, line, ht);
22.             break;
23.         default:
24.             zend_output_debug_string(1, "%s(%d) : ht=%p is inconsistent", file, line, ht);
25.             break;
26.     }
27.     zend_bailout();
28. }
29. #define IS_CONSISTENT(a) _zend_is_inconsistent(a, __FILE__, __LINE__);
30. #define SET_INCONSISTENT(n) do { \
31.         HT_FLAGS(ht) = (HT_FLAGS(ht) & ~HASH_FLAG_CONSISTENCY) | (n); \
32.     } while (0)
33. #else
34. #define IS_CONSISTENT(a)
35. #define SET_INCONSISTENT(n)
36. #endif
```

A glance at the code indicates we're doing some sanity checking when deleting (destroying) the hash table and releasing its memory. PHP garbage collection can potentially have several phases, but that's a discussion for another time. Right now we're looking for the pattern.

Line 1 is #if ZEND_DEBUG, and the last four lines contain the else and endif. It is a compile-time check. The choice is made when compiling PHP. We can't run PHP with checking on one time and off another. We'd need to recompile PHP with ZEND_DEBUG defined or not defined.

The function _zend_is_inconsistent only gets compiled with the debug flag on. Without ZEND_DEBUG, the function won't exist at all. With debugging on, the IS_CONSISTENT(ht) macro does the checking, passing in the file name and line number for display purposes.

With debug off, the macro compiles to nothing. The macro becomes empty white space. Our line of code gets reduced to the semicolon ;. Fortunately, an empty statement is legal C code. Multiple empty statements ; ; ; are perfectly legal, just like with PHP.

Lines 30-32 show another common idiom: do { ... } while (0). Here the macro is introducing a block of code. A do block executes at least once, just like with PHP. The while(0) ensures it executes only once.

However, unlike PHP, a variable can be declared inside that do block, and its scope is only inside that block. In PHP, the variable is available anywhere inside the function/method, but in C it's limited to the nearest enclosing set of braces. In a macro, the do block technique allows the macro to stick multiple lines of C code pretty much anywhere, complete with temporary variables that disappear at the end of the macro.

These code insertion techniques can be maddening to follow, but they provide a consistent way of source code generation. The compiler then takes the ugly result and compiles it into the most efficient code it can.

In a #define, the backslash \ at the end of the line says the definition continues on the next line.

Again, the detail of the IS_CONSISTENT(ht) macro doesn't matter. What's important is recognizing the pattern so you can understand what's happening without tripping over the details. The PHP virtual machine, C code, gets generated by a PHP script. So, unlike standard PHP source code, much of the Zend Engine (runtime PHP compiler/interpreter) isn't handcrafted like we might expect.

Reference Count

Listing 8.5 line 8 reads HT_ASSERT_RC1(ht);. We know the pattern, so we can make some guesses. The answers, if you're interested, are at Zend/zend_hash.c near line 30. "Asserts" tend to be active only in debug mode. Sure enough, without debug mode, this macro compiles down to empty space.

The PHP compiler uses reference counts for various entities. When the reference count drops to zero, perhaps as a result of unset($variable) in your PHP code, the item's memory can be released and reused (in the "garbage collection" phase). In PHP, for example, if you have two variables both pointing to the same object instance, that object might have a reference count of two. You'd have to unset both variables before that object can safely disappear.

With HT_ASSERT_RC1(ht), the HT_ prefix is used all over the hash table feature code. The pointer to the hash table is often a variable named ht. So we can pretty well guess this is a sanity check (used in debug mode only) that our hash table has a reference count of one. The hash table is the internal representation of one specific array. The hash table code is written in such a way that the reference count is *always* one. So the sanity check makes sense.

Packed Hash Table

An ordered list of values such as [1, 1, 2, 3, 5, 8] is a special case. The array keys are consecutive integers beginning with 0. PHP (written in C) stores the array as a packed hash table. The array value is stored in that Bucket we've been discussing. We either store the value directly if it's small enough (int, float, or bool), or we store the pointer to the separate slab of memory containing that value.

Remember, the array is actually the ordered set of key-value pairs:

```
[0 => 1, 1 => 1, 2 => 2, 3 => 3, 4 => 5, 5 => 8]
```

We store key/value *n* in bucket *n*. $array[0] is in bucket 0; array[4] is in bucket 4, and so on. It's simple and efficient.

If the array is not a "packed" array, it's more difficult to find which bucket contains our array element. We transform the array key through a hashing function to find a possible bucket number. More than one key could hash to the same bucket number. So we check that *possible* bucket to see if it is the right key. If not, we follow its link to the next possible bucket, and so on down the collision chain until we find the matching key or fail completely (the array key does not exist).

Listing 8.5 line 9 reads ZEND_ASSERT(!(HT_FLAGS(ht) & HASH_FLAG_PACKED));. The ASSERT is no doubt a sanity check only active in debug mode. The answer is in Zend/zend_portability.h near line 100. What's interesting to us is the FLAG pattern. It's important to recognize and understand.

However, first, let's note the overall intent of this line. We're asserting that the "packed" flag is not set. This function (line 1 of the listing) aims to find a bucket given the array key. The array key is a string, so we definitely should not be dealing with a packed hash table. The packed hash table is only used for that particular case of continuous numeric keys beginning with zero.

Line 9 includes a Boolean NOT, a bitwise AND, and a hidden bitwise left shift. It's a typical pattern throughout the source code, so let's dive down that rabbit hole.

Flags

The HT_FLAGS macro is near line 43 of Zend/zend_hash.h.

```
#define HASH_FLAG_CONSISTENCY        ((1<<0) | (1<<1))
#define HASH_FLAG_PACKED             (1<<2)
#define HASH_FLAG_UNINITIALIZED      (1<<3)
#define HASH_FLAG_STATIC_KEYS        (1<<4) /* long and interned strings */
#define HASH_FLAG_HAS_EMPTY_IND      (1<<5)
#define HASH_FLAG_ALLOW_COW_VIOLATION (1<<6)

#define HT_FLAGS(ht) (ht)->u.flags
```

We know from the function signature (Listing 8.5 line 1) that ht is a pointer of type HashTable. The next listing is Zend/zend_types.h near line 235. See Listing 8.8.

Listing 8.8 Zend/zend_types extract

```
1. typedef struct _zend_array HashTable;
2.
3. struct _zend_array {
4.     zend_refcounted_h gc;
5.     union {
6.         struct {
7.             ZEND_ENDIAN_LOHI_4(
8.                 zend_uchar    flags,
9.                 zend_uchar    _unused,
10.                zend_uchar    nIteratorsCount,
11.                zend_uchar    _unused2)
12.        } v;
13.        uint32_t flags;
14.    } u;
15.    uint32_t        nTableMask;
16.    Bucket          *arData;
17.    uint32_t        nNumUsed;
18.    uint32_t        nNumOfElements;
19.    uint32_t        nTableSize;
20.    uint32_t        nInternalPointer;
21.    zend_long        nNextFreeElement;
22.    dtor_func_t      pDestructor;
23. };
```

Well, now. We have quite a rabbit hole. Again, this is typical. As you learn the codebase you'll be chasing down one topic after another. The style of code, though, is consistent—and that's the point. As you come to recognize the patterns, terse as they are, you'll recognize the code's structure in those patterns.

That's the whole point here: recognizing and understanding those patterns. That's your key to not being intimidated by the terseness and opaqueness of the code. Your comfort level, and your confidence level, will increase. Meanwhile, we have this rabbit hole to explore.

Line 1 says that HashTable is a synonym for _zend_array. I'm guessing a lot of other things are also synonyms for _zend_array. No doubt that's why the typedef and the struct are declared separately.

We only care about u.flags, but let's take a peek at some other things while we're here. gc stands for "garbage collection." It includes reference counts. "Endian" is a macro allowing for the fact that different computers have different endianness[42]. Some computers store stuff in memory front-to-back, and other computers store stuff inside-out and backward. The ZEND_ENDIAN macros ensure that things get laid-out in memory consistently across various architectures.

In C, a union is what you'd expect. Fields v and flags are accessed at the same memory location. Remember, in C, a variable (or field) is just a pointer to a memory location. C is perfectly happy to treat those 32 bits as a whole set of flags, or something with an "iterators count" stuffed in the middle. If you want the 8-bit nIteratorsCount, access it as u.v.nIteratorsCount. If you want the 32 bits of flags, access them as u.flags.

Note the rest of the fields (other than arData) are plain values, not pointers. The plain value might be a pointer, such as pDestructor, but that's the programmer's issue and not ours at the moment.

arData will point to that slab of memory we've been describing. For bucket n, the memory offset is n times sizeof(Bucket) in bytes. arData plus that memory offset is a pointer to bucket n. As we saw earlier, that slab of memory also contains hash results at a negative offset. arData actually points into the middle of that slab of memory.

HASH_FLAG_PACKED is (1<<2) which is 4. Our FLAGS macros are dealing with bit fields packed into a single variable. We extract the single flag with the bitwise AND (&). We test for zero/nonzero as true/false. The NOT operator negates the result.

Why do we use (1<<2) instead of just saying 4? This operation is common with bit fields all defined in the same variable. The number is the bit number being used. We can see at a glance that bits 0..6 (counting the rightmost, least-significant, bit as bit 0) are in use. If someone needed to define another bit field, clearly (1<<7) is the next available field.

Isn't specifying the left shift less efficient than just specifying the value 1, 2, 4, 8, and so on? No, it isn't. The compiler does the calculation at compile time. It performs the substitution for us. It's better to do it this way for readability's sake.

When we're dealing with, say, 24 bits, it's easy to make a mistake. Which bit is 131072? What if we accidentally wrote it as 131272? Would a reviewer catch that? Using hexadecimal might avoid that problem. 0x40000 has only one bit set, but which bit, counting from zero? We've been talking about bit 16, 17, 18—which bit did we mean? In the context of a sequence of bit-flag definitions, (1<<17) makes sense—once we recognize and understand the pattern.

Finally, take a look at Listing 8.5 line 18, HT_FLAGS(ht) &= ~HASH_FLAG_STATIC_KEYS;. We know from the header file HASH_FLAG_STATIC_KEYS is (1<<4), which is 16, but let's call it bit 4.

---

[42] endianness: https://en.wikipedia.org/wiki/Endianness

The ~ operator works just like PHP. Flip all the bits. All bits that are 1 become 0, and all that are 0 become 1. Therefore, ~16 means that all bits *except* bit 4 are set to 1.

"Anything" ANDed with 1 is the same "anything." In this case ht->u.flags ANDed with ~16 leaves all of the flags intact except bit 4. Anything ANDed with 0 is 0. Therefore, what this is doing is clearing bit 4 to zero and leaving everything else as-is. We don't know, at this point, why we're clearing the static keys flag, but we can now recognize the pattern for clearing a bit-flag. When you see this pattern, the code is clearing a flag (or a subfield within a field).

The opposite pattern for setting a bit flag looks like this:

```
HT_FLAGS(ht) |= HASH_FLAG_STATIC_KEYS;
```

Any value ORed with 0 is the same value. Anything ORed with 1 is 1. So we're leaving the other flags as-is and setting the static keys flag to 1.

The above line of code appears to have a function call as the left side of an assignment statement. That wouldn't be legal PHP code, and it's not legal C code either. We're looking at a macro evaluated at compile time. The fact that it's all upper case is our clue that it's a macro. A macro is purely a text substitution.

After substitution, the C compiler will see:

```
(ht)->u.flags |= (1<<4);
```

We can now see the line of perfectly legal C code. We can see what it does. On the other hand, now that we know the pattern, the "macro" form more clearly expresses the intent. The macros aim to show us what the code is trying to accomplish.

Summary

The PHP compiler/interpreter is written in C. The C syntax itself is quite similar to PHP's syntax. Thus, in theory, it's relatively easy to read the C code and see how it works—it's the context and environment that presents the challenge. We hit that challenge head-on.

We looked at how to create an executable file, and how to tell one from the other. Sometimes the weirdness needs to be traced back to its historical setting to be understood.

We focused on the theory of hash tables because that's how PHP stores arrays. The PHP arrays were our focus for this deep dive. We first looked at "packed" hash tables in detail. The "packed" hash table is a PHP concept using the idea of a perfect hashing function.

The general hash table is a key-value store. PHP takes this concept further, declaring PHP arrays to be *ordered* hash tables.

We use the hashing function for string keys to create an integer hash. Where the array key is an integer, we use that integer as the hash.

Given the hash value, we map that value to a hash slot. The hash slot contains the bucket number of the first bucket of our collision chain. We follow the collision chain from bucket to bucket until finding the bucket we seek or hitting the end of the chain (array key not found).

When the hash table contains holes, we compact the hash table by moving the buckets down to use the holes, and recalculating the map of bucket slots. We call that "rehashing" the table.

Now that we understood how hash tables work with PHP (written in C), we began looking at the implementation in C. We looked for, and learned, idioms and patterns in the C codebase.

We learned about how macros, structs, and typedefs are used in the C code. PHP (written in C) often stores information (flags) as bit fields. We saw examples of the macros examining, setting, and clearing those bit fields.

Chapter

Impostor Syndrome

We have yet to acknowledge the elephant in the room. Impostor syndrome and the related concerns affect a large proportion of us in the high-technology ecosystem. Here's my own story regarding impostor syndrome. We wrap this chapter up with the reminder that skills, and understanding, both come from practice.

What Is Impostor Syndrome?

Megan Dalla-Camina explains for *Psychology Today*[1]:

> *The impostor syndrome is a psychological term referring to a pattern of behavior where people doubt their accomplishments and have a persistent, often internalized fear of being exposed as a fraud. Not an actual disorder, the term was coined by clinical psychologists Pauline Clance and Suzanne Imes in 1978, when they found that despite having adequate external evidence of accomplishments, people with impostor syndrome remained convinced that they don't deserve the success they have.*

Software Training

Throughout this project to share *The Fizz Buzz Fix*, I've been asking myself, "Who am I to be writing this book?" I'm not a superstar who should be teaching you how to think like an expert software developer. I keep reminding myself that nobody else has taken quite this approach, and that, therefore, the way is open for me to do so.

I was strongly affected by impostor syndrome from roughly age 10 through age 30. Impostor syndrome told me that, since I'd been studying computers longer than anyone else around me, that I had to be better than *everyone* else around me. You'll laugh, because you know it doesn't work that way.

Midway through college I transferred from the United States Air Force Academy to the University of Washington. That had nothing to do with impostor syndrome; rather, it was clear I didn't want a military career, and by that point, I was nearing the bottom of my class.

I departed the University of Washington mid-way through my senior year in the Department of Computer Science. That *was* impostor syndrome, though I didn't realize it at the time. My attitude was horrible by this point so I left school to get a job in the computer industry, which is where I thought I'd want to be, and see if I liked it. I started with Cray Research and 20 years later remained with the same company and the same industry.

For what it's worth, I think I know where my impostor syndrome originated—or at least began to. Let me share my story to help your own career path.

---

[1] *Psychology Today:* https://phpa.me/dalla-camina-impostor-syndrome

Training the Trainer

My first day (and first six weeks) with Cray Research was the first day of the next six-week training sequence. It was the only way to get trained on a CRAY-1 since fewer than a dozen actually existed at that time.

Six years later, I joined the Software Training department to teach the operating system internals. To that point, the various instructors had formal teaching experience and needed to learn the subject matter well enough to teach it. With me, they flipped it the other way around. We all thought it a worthwhile experiment to bring in a subject matter expert and teach me to teach; it worked out well. The students sent to be trained in operating system internals at Cray Research were something like the movie *Top Gun* (1986). They were "the best of the best" and thus the instructors needed to be subject-matter experts.

I sat through the now eight-week training sequence—the new I/O Subsystem's existence tacked on the additional two weeks—that culminated in a class project. I was the rookie, the new member of the Software Training staff. I was supposed to be a subject matter expert, but who would know?

I asked around. Nope, nobody had considered writing an adventure game as their "hello world" project. That would be unreasonable; we were just being exposed to the I/O Subsystem machine instructions for the first time. This was bare-metal programming in assembly language. Anything much larger than Hello World required considerable memory management—and the I/O Subsystem had its own memory management libraries to be learned.

We learned about the Hello World assignment the first day of the two-week I/O Subsystem Software course. Mind you, "hello world" is not as easy as it might sound. "Hello world" meant building a new channel driver in the operating system. The operator console was on a hard-wired I/O channel with interrupts, channel priorities, and so on. This was a "capstone" assignment completing the eight weeks of instruction.

I used the two weeks to plan out Swiss Adventure and design its maze of twisty little passages[2]. This wasn't about being a "gamer;" this was my plan for establishing credibility as the incoming rookie instructor. My bid for credibility worked; no student had ever written such a complex program inside the I/O Subsystem.

There was one more piece to the preparation. The previous two-week course had been operating system internals for the Cray mainframe. I would be teaching this class.

The class includes an operating system printout, a "memory dump" in octal. This is the memory (what we now call RAM) contents as of when the operating system crashed,

---

[2]   *maze of twisty little passages:* https://en.wikipedia.org/wiki/Colossal_Cave_Adventure

containing the operating system's in-memory data structures and event traces. As an example, here's the page from our training workbook explaining the history trace format. See Figure 9.1.

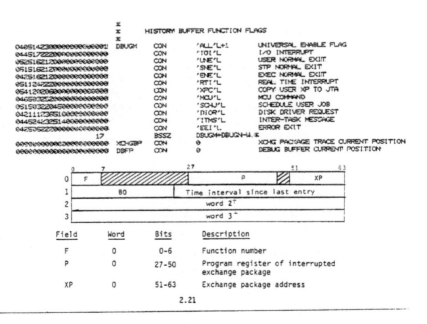

Figure 9.1. Kernel History Trace Format

Here's a page of that history trace from the CRAY-1 memory dump, formatted according to the layout shown in the previous image. See Figure 9.2.

The class, as you can imagine, was excruciating, studying hundreds of pages of octal numbers. But there was no way around it. Meanwhile, the software instructors had a problem to solve.

The printed training workbooks needed to remain relevant and bit-for-bit correct from one software release to the next. We needed to trigger the *same* system crash from one software release to the next. We reprinted the crash dump anew for each release, and updated source code listings—yes, on paper— but kept the workbook diagrams and explanations the same, except for feature updates.

We changed one line of code, which corrupted memory. It mistakenly stored ASCII text in a memory word that was supposed to be a set of processing flags. Each trip through the operating system main loop, the operating system checked the flags and ran the task indicated by that flag, clearing the flag upon completion of that task.

```
AUTO - SYSTEM DUMP AUTOMATIC FORMATTING          FDUMP 1.02      11/28/79   11:44:44   PAGE   43


FUNCTION   P-REG      SAVED B0     XP      INTERVAL                      WORDS 2 AND 3

011  DGM    0001660A   0000001B    01500   0000000000472   0114400000202710007/0220 0400000000000000000000      @
011  DGM    0001660A   0000001E    01500   0000000000276   0000010011110001450000 0000000002560000002557      @
001  I/O    0001660A   0327760A    01500   0000000003050   0000050000230300067053 0000000000000041777777      +
001  I/O    0001660A   0327760A    01500   0000000000073   0000050000230300067173 0000000000000041777777
001  I/O    0001660A   0327760A    01500   0000000000501   0000040000230300067212 0000000000000041777777
001  I/O    0001660A   0327760A    01500   0000000002340   0000050000230300067856 0100000000000041777777
001  I/O    0001660A   0327760A    01500   0000000000714   0000050000230300066274 0100000000000041777777
001  I/O    0001660A   0327760A    01500   0000000000612   0000040000230300066325 0100000000000041777777
001  I/O    0001660A   0327760A    01500   0000000000774   0000050000230300067755 0100000000000041001177
001  I/O    0001660A   0327760A    01500   0000000001122   0000050000230300070167 0100000000000041001177
010  SCP    0001660A   0000000A    01500   0000000000777   0000000000000000000000 0013001265000777771500      +P  @
004  ENE    0001660A   0001461C    01500   0000000000364   0000000000000000000000 0013001265000777771500      +P  @
001  I/O    0001660C   0327760A    01500   0000000003735   0000050000230300070220 0100000000000041001177
011  DGM    0001660C   0000001B    01500   0000000000472   0114400000202710007/0220 0400000000000000000000      @
011  DGM    0001660C   0000001B    01500   0000000000276   0000010011110001450000 0000000002560000002557      @
001  I/O    0001660C   0327760A    01500   0000000003050   0000050000230300067053 0000000000000041777777      +
001  I/O    0001660C   0327760A    01500   0000000000073   0000050000230300067173 0000000000000041777777
001  I/O    0001660C   0327760A    01500   0000000000501   0000040000230300067212 0000000000000041777777
001  I/O    0001660C   0327760A    01500   0000000002340   0000050000230300067856 0100000000000041777777
001  I/O    0001660C   0327760A    01500   0000000000714   0000050000230300066274 0100000000000041777777
001  I/O    0001660C   0327760A    01500   0000000000612   0000040000230300066325 0100000000000041777777
001  I/O    0001660C   0327760A    01500   0000000000774   0000050000230300067755 0100000000000041001177
001  I/O    0001660C   0327760A    01500   0000000001122   0000050000230300070167 0100000000000041001177
010  SCP    0001660C   0000000A    01500   0000000000777   0000000000000000000000 0013001265000777771500      +P  @
004  ENE    0001660C   0001461C    01500   0000000000364   0000000000000000000000 0013001265000777771500      +P  @
001  I/O    0001652C   0327760A    01500   0000000003735   0000040000230300070220 0100000000000041001177
011  DGM    0001652C   0000001B    01500   0000000000472   0114400000202710007/0220 0400000000000000000000      @
011  DGM    0001652C   0000001B    01500   0000000000276   0000010011110001450000 0000000002560000002557      @
001  I/O    0001652C   0327760A    01500   0000000003050   0000050000230300067053 0000000000000041777777      +
001  I/O    0001652C   0327760A    01500   0000000000073   0000050000230300067173 0000000000000041777777
001  I/O    0001652C   0327760A    01500   0000000000501   0000040000230300067212 0000000000000041777777
001  RTI    0001652C   0000000C    01500   0000000002025   1000000000000000000000 0013001265000777771500      +P  @
001  DNE    0101636D   0101676A    02060   0000000001345   0000000000000000001650 0013001265000777771500      +P  @
001  RTI    0050606B   0102432B    02060   0000000000456   0000000000000000001650 0013001265000777771500      +P  @
003  SHE    0050606B   0102472B    02060   0000000000753   0000000202020200000714 0000000000000001212020
012  ITM    0050606B   0102432B    02060   0000000000250   1000000000307000033333 0000000000000000036610      @ 6       =
```

Figure 9.2. Kernel Trace

The operating system eventually crashed, detecting it was executing code that shouldn't be executed given the current context. The crash gave no clue as to the real cause of the problem.

The CRAY-1 has machine instructions allowing the programmer to, say, set address 1234 into address register A1 and then load or store from/to memory using that base address as the offset. To cause our crash we took a similar situation and inserted a line of code that cleared the address register to zero just before storing a status value as ASCII characters into memory. The instructor who came up with that idea was diabolical. They arranged for that ASCII text to be stored in the operating system "processing needed" flags field (one of several such fields).

As the operating system processed each flag, mistakenly, which led to the crash, it cleared the flags one by one. By the time the crash happened and we printed out the memory dump, the ASCII text was no longer visible. The operating system had cleared it out, bit by bit, erasing the evidence. Diabolical.

So here I was sitting through the class sequence. At some point during those two weeks I realized what was happening and traced the order of events that matched which flags were clear and which were not, and reconstructed the ASCII text. That led me to the inserted line of code; I showed the instructor what I'd found, and the sequence of events in the main loop that led to the crash. He said no prior student had ever found the root cause of their crash used for training purposes. I was the rookie instructor and that had been my other minor point of establishing credibility. I found the root cause because of my experience. I knew how to work my way through those operating system dumps, work through the event traces line by line, compare to the data structures, and so on.

I found the root cause because I actually was a subject matter expert. But I remained the rookie instructor. Impostor syndrome was still asking, "Who am I to be teaching this stuff when everyone else has years of practice teaching this material?"

Promoted to Instructor

When the next sequence came around, the boss put me on the schedule to teach it. I said I wasn't ready—I didn't yet know the material well enough to teach it. The boss felt I should be ready since I'd just taken two months sitting through the *entire* sequence. We compromised; I would teach part of the material. That meant I could study-up on those specific parts and placate my impostor syndrome.

Each student gets about two shelf-feet of manuals in three-ring binders as reference material for the two-week class. Those manuals come with countless "change packets," the few (or many) changed pages for each operating system release. We can lose the first hour or more of class having students break open the shrink-wrapped manuals, get them into three-ring binders, and apply the change packets one by one.

So, instead, the instructor spends a full weekend day setting up class—in particular, preparing the set of manuals for each student. Weekends were the only option because the classroom was in use during the week.

The boss called me on Saturday. The assigned instructor had been involved in an accident and was in hospital for at least a week—he fully recovered eventually. I would need to teach the class, and that also meant I needed to do the set-up. Setting it up was no problem. But two weeks of operating system internals, in pure raw octal and assembly language, starting Monday morning? There were no other options.

Remember, people were coming to learn to program "a CRAY." Companies and government agencies sent their best and most senior people—the ones who could handle working with a new hardware instruction set, understood what channel drivers do, and so on. I was to be the face of Cray Research to these people. I was the youngest person in the room by far; I was expected to be the expert. Impostor syndrome said I wasn't ready but the boss said we had no other options.

On Friday afternoon, two weeks later with the course instruction completed, I explained to the class that I'd step out of the room and the boss would come in to solicit feedback. We did that for all classes. I explained this was my first time teaching the course, that it happened unexpectedly, and I'd greatly appreciate any feedback or suggestions at all for better teaching the course next time around. People were surprised to hear it was my first time teaching. I was surprised they were surprised! But we had gotten along well, as one "Real Programmer" to another, so to speak.

That's a useful lesson in itself; when it's your first time presenting, *don't tell anyone!* Thirty years later, at my first conference talk, I kept that fact a secret. People had no idea, so telling would have been distracting.

The boss solicited verbal feedback and handed out our standard paper survey with a series of questions with ratings 1-5, with 5 being the top rating. I received across-the-board straight fives from every person. I had unwittingly stacked the deck in my favor!

Less of an Impostor

I tell you this story because that's where the impostor syndrome began to lose its grip. It was okay that the other instructors were more experienced than I. That didn't make me an impostor, though it felt like it. I was teaching how the operating system worked even though those writing the software in the Software Division knew more about it than I did. My students consistently had far more experience than me, but I represented Cray Research to them. I felt like an impostor, but I wasn't.

Impostor syndrome, for me, doesn't care whether I happen to know as much, or have as much experience, as someone else. Impostor syndrome expects me to have as much experience as, and know as much as, *everyone* else all put together.

I have felt terrible for two months now, writing this book as if I'm the expert. I pretended to be the expert so you'd hopefully listen to what I had to say. I've literally been telling myself for months that nobody else wrote it, so it's okay if I do.

It took me 20 years to get past impostor syndrome and, 30 years later, it's obviously still with me. That's why I keep repeating "pay it forward." When I *can* pay it forward, Impostor syndrome can be set aside. I can avoid worrying about whether I am the best person to be paying it forward; I just do it whether I'm the best person to do so or not.

Resources

We have many people in the tech industry affected by impostor syndrome, anxiety, depression, and other issues related to mental wellness. We don't hear it much because saying anything can affect our employment prospects.

Ed Finkler began speaking at tech conferences about his personal experiences as a web developer and open source advocate with a mental health disorder. The response was overwhelming. A *large* proportion of us in the tech industry are affected one way or another. (See the Mental Health in Tech Surveys[3] from 2014-present.) Thus, *Open Sourcing Mental Illness* (OSMI) was born. Their website[4] includes education, resources, research. The purpose? *Create a workplace that nurtures and supports mental wellness.*

When I first contacted Parisa Tabriz asking permission to quote her article *So you want to work in security?* she responded, "Sure," and attached a graphic that is the best explanation of impostor syndrome I've ever encountered. How did she know? (She works for Google, so I may have just answered my own question.) She clearly knows this and related issues are that common in our industry. The article is *Combatting the impostor syndrome in academic science—you probably are as smart as they think!*[5]. Be sure to read Parisa's own advice in *So, you want to work in security?*[6].

---

[3] Mental Health in Tech Surveys: https://osmihelp.org/research
[4] website: https://osmihelp.org
[5] Combatting the impostor syndrome in academic science—you probably are as smart as they think!: https://phpa.me/combatting-impostor-syndrome/
[6] So, you want to work in security?: https://phpa.me/work-in-security

A closely-related concern is when we observe someone who "makes it look easy," whatever "it" happens to be. Azeria, in laying out *The Process of Mastering a Skill*[7], writes:

> *Prodigy or expert? Have you ever wondered what separates experts from everyone else? I don't mean the self-proclaimed "experts" who value status over learning. I mean the "geniuses" of our industry who know their field extraordinarily well and have spent decades honing their skills. How do these successful researchers master their field? Is it some natural talent they were born with, or do they have a magic trick that only a few know about? When performance psychologists studied what distinguishes experts across several different fields, they kept coming across the same answer in each field: deliberate practice.*

Azeria distills a lifetime of learning and mastery into that one article. Your minutes reading her voice of experience will be well spent.

Actor David Carradine played the role of Kwai Chang Caine in the TV series *Kung Fu*[8] (1972-1975). "Part of the appeal of the series was undoubtedly the emphasis laid, via flashbacks, on the mental and spiritual power that Caine had gained from his rigorous training." In these flashbacks, Master Po calls his young student "Grasshopper" in reference to a scene from the pilot episode:

> **Master Po:** *Close your eyes. What do you hear?*
>
> **Young Caine:** *I hear the water, I hear the birds.*
>
> **Po:** *Do you hear your own heartbeat?*
>
> **Caine:** *No.*
>
> **Po:** *Do you hear the grasshopper which is at your feet?*
>
> **Caine:** *Old man, how is it that you hear these things?*
>
> **Po:** *Young man, how is it that you do not?*

Our current days are really no different from the "good old days" that were really not so good after all. The details will continue to evolve, but what we do remains both an art and a science. Chart your own path. Plan and prepare, and practice.

You'll do well.

---

[7] *The Process of Mastering a Skill:* https://phpa.me/azeria-mastering-skill
[8] *Kung Fu:* https://phpa.me/wikip-kung-fu-tv

Index

php[architect] Books

The php[architect] series of books cover topics relevant to modern PHP programming. We offer our books in both print and digital formats. Print copy price includes free shipping to the US. Books sold digitally are available to you DRM-free in PDF, ePub, or Mobi formats for viewing on any device that supports these.

To view the complete selection of books and order a copy of your own, please visit: http://phparch.com/books/.

- **The Dev Lead Trenches: Lessons for Managing Developers**
  By Chris Tankersley
  ISBN: 978-1940111711

- **Web Scraping with PHP, 2nd Edition**
  By Matthew Turland
  ISBN: 978-1940111674

- **Security Principles for PHP Applications**
  By Eric Mann
  ISBN: 978-1940111612

- **Docker for Developers, 2nd Edition**
  By Chris Tankersley
  ISBN: 978-1940111568 (Print edition)

- **What's Next? Professional Development Advice**
  Edited by Oscar Merida
  ISBN: 978-1940111513

- **Functional Programing in PHP, 2nd Edition**
  By: Simon Holywell
  ISBN: 978-1940111469

- **Web Security 2016**
  Edited by Oscar Merida
  ISBN: 978-1940111414

- **Building Exceptional Sites with WordPress & Thesis**
  By Peter MacIntyre
  ISBN: 978-1940111315

- **Integrating Web Services with OAuth and PHP**
  By Matthew Frost
  ISBN: 978-1940111261

- **Zend Framework 1 to 2 Migration Guide**
  By Bart McLeod
  ISBN: 978-1940111216

- **XML Parsing with PHP**
  By John M. Stokes
  ISBN: 978-1940111162

- **Zend PHP 5 Certification Study Guide, Third Edition**
  By Davey Shafik with Ben Ramsey
  ISBN: 978-1940111100

- **Mastering the SPL Library**
  By Joshua Thijssen
  ISBN: 978-1940111001

Feedback and Updates

Please let us know what you thought of this book! What did you enjoy? What was confusing or could have been improved? Did you find errata? Any feedback and thoughts you have regarding this book will help us improve a future edition.

To leave a review, go to https://phpa.me/fizzbuzz-book

Follow the Author

Edward Barnard is active on twitter, @ewbarnard, and shares other experiences, lessons, and stories like the ones in this book frequently.

Updates

To keep in touch and be notified about future editions to this book, visit http://phparch.com and sign up for our (low-volume) mailing list.

You can also follow us on twitter @phparch as well as on facebook: https://facebook.com/phparch/

Printed in Great Britain
by Amazon

44463274R00113